The

Year

of the

Poet VII

May 2020

The Poetry Posse

inner child press, ltd.

The Poetry Posse 2020

Gail Weston Shazor

Shareef Abdur Rasheed

Teresa E. Gallion

hülya n. yılmaz

Kimberly Burnham

Tzemin Ition Tsai

Elizabeth Esguerra Castillo

Jackie Davis Allen

Joe Paire

Caroline 'Ceri' Nazareno

Ashok K. Bhargava

Alicja Maria Kuberska

Swapna Behera

Albert 'Infinite' Carrasco

Eliza Segiet

William S. Peters, Sr.

~ * ~

In order to maintain each poet's authentic voice, this volume has not undergone the scrutiny of editing. Please take time to indulge each contributor for their own creativity and aspirations to convey their uniqueness.

hülya n. yılmaz, Ph.D.
Director of Editing
Inner Child Press International

General Information

The Year of the Poet VII
May 2020 Edition

The Poetry Posse

1st Edition : 2020

Publisher Information
1st Edition : Inner Child Press
intouch@innerchildpress.com
www.innerchildpress.com

ISBN-13 : 978-1-952081-15-6 (inner child press, ltd.)

$ 12.99

WHAT WOULD LIFE BE WITHOUT A LITTLE POETRY?

Dedication

This Book is dedicated to

Humanity, Peace & Poetry

the Power of the Pen

can effectuate change!

&

The Poetry Posse

past, present & future

our Patrons and Readers

the Spirit of our Everlasting Muse

In the darkness of my life
I heard the music
I danced . . .
and the Light appeared
and I dance

Janet P. Caldwell

Table of Contents

The Poetry Posse

Table of Contents . . . *continued*

May's Featured Poets   111

Inner Child News   141

Other Anthological Works   167

Foreword

Ralph Bunche
(b. Aug. 07 1904, d. Dec. 09 1971

Ralph Bunche was a renown American political
scientist and diplomat. He was Nobel Peace Prize
recipient for his work in the Middle East in the late
1940's negotiating to bring peace between Egypt
and Israel. In 1950 he became the first African
American to be awarded the honor. Born in Detroit
in 1904 and after the family relocated over the years
several times they settled in Los Angeles, CA.
Bunche was a excellent student and was
valedictorian of his high school graduating class
and his UCLA class as well. He earned a graduate
scholarship to attend Harvard University and his
South-Central LA community raised money to help
him in that pursuit where he went on to earning a
Masters and Doctorate (PHD) in Political Science.
On the way to earning that he was teaching political
science at Howard University a major Black school.
He also published his first book World view of Race
in 1936. Ralph Bunche served as chairman of
Howard's Political Science Department. for more
than two decades (1928 to 1950). During WW2 he
was with the Office of Strategic Services (OSS) the
wartime intelligence service as a senior social
analyst on Colonial Affairs. in 1943 he was
transferred to the State Dept. He was appointed

Associate Chief of the Division of Dependent Area Affairs.

UNITED NATIONS

Ralph Bunche was with the United Nations (U.N.) 25 years. He participated in the preliminary planning for the U.N. At the San Francisco Conference of 1945. He was instrumental in the creation and adoption of the Universal Declaration of Human Rights.

NOBEL PEACE PRIZE

In 1947 he was involved in the negotiations to resolve the Arab-Israeli conflict. Eventually he became the principal negotiator and through his skillful diplomatic efforts was credited playing a major role in reaching a agreement through the 1949 Armistice Agreement. Prior to the agreement Bunche had a potter create memorial plates to be presented to each negotiator. One of them was the representative for Israel Moshe Dayan who was known to discuss issues relating to the conflict with Bunche over a game of pool. Later he approached Bunche after the agreement was reached and the plates were given to the negotiators and asked him what if the talks fell through after you had the plates made. Bunche replied " I'd have broken them over your dam heads". This accomplishment lead to Bunche being awarded the Nobel Peace Prize in 1950. Ralph Bunche in addition to the Arab-Israeli conflict mediated in many others in his years as a diplomat and negotiator with the United Nations including The Congo, Yeman, Kashmir and Cyprus to name a few.

CIVIL RIGHTS

Ralph Bunche not only played major roles in resolving international crisis but locally he played a significant role in the Civil Rights Movement of the 50's and 60's in the United States. He participated in the March on Washington in 1963 when Rev, Martin Luther King gave his famous 'I have a Dream ' speech and the march from Selma to Montgomery, Alabama in 1965. Ralph Bunche received the coveted Presidential Medal of freedom from President John Kennedy in 1963. His amazing work during the 25 years with the U.N. was encapsulated in the United Nations document, Ralph Bunche: Visionary for Peace.

"He championed the principle of equal rights for everyone, regardless of race or creed. He believed in 'the essential goodness of all people, and that no problem in human relations is insoluble.' Through the UN Trusteeship Council, Bunche readied the international stage for a period of rapid transformation, dismantling the old colonial systems in Africa and Asia, and guiding scores of emerging nations through the transition to independence in the post-war era ".

Shareef Abdur-Rasheed AKA Zakir Flo,
Poetry Posse, ICPI

World Healing World Peace
2020

Poets for Humanity

Now Available

www.innerchildpress.com/world-healing-world-peace-poetry

www.worldhealingworldpeacepoetry.com

www.worldhealingworldpeacefoundation.org

Preface

Yes I am excited and feel accomplished as we enter our seventh year of publishing what I and many others deem to be a worthy enterprise, *The Year of the Poet*.

This past year we have aligned our vision with that of Nober Peace Prize Recipients. We have title this year's theme. The Year of Peace! Hopefully thorugh our sharing each month, our poetry can have a profound effect on our global consciousness and the need for peace while educating ourselves and our readership about some of the individuals who have made history through their efforts to promulgate peace for all of humanity.. We are on our way to hitting yet another milestone. Needless to say, I am elated.

To reiterate, our initial vision was to just perform at this level for the year of 2014. Since that time we have had the blessed opportunity to include many other wonderful poets, word artists and storytellers in the Poetry Posse from lands, cultures and persuasions all over the world. We have featured hundreds of additional poets, thereby introducing their poetic offerings to our vast global audience.

In keeping with our effort and vision to expand the awareness of poets from all walks by making this offerings accessible, we at Inner Child Press International will continue to make every volume a FREE Download. The books are also available for purchase at the affordable cost of $7.00 per volume.

In the previous years, our monthly themes were Flowers, Birds, Gemstones, Trees and Past Cultures. This coming year we have elected to continue our focus of choosing what we consider a significant subject . . . PEACE! In each month's volume you will have the opportunity to not only read at least one poem themed by our Poetry Posse members about such celebrated Peace Ambassadors, but we have included a few words about each individual in our prologue. We hope you find the poetic offerings insightful as we use our poetic form to relay to you what we too have learned through our research in making our offering available to you, our readership.

In closing, we would like to thank you for being an integral part of our amazing journey.

Enjoy our amazing featured poets . . . they are amazing!

Building Cultural Bridges of Understanding . . .

Bless Up . . . From the home in our hearts to yours

Bill

The Poetry Posse
Inner Child Press Ineternational

PS

Do Not forget about the World Healing, World Peace Poetry effort.

Available here

www.worldhealingworldpeacepoetry.com

**For Free Downloads of Previous Issues of
The Year of the Poet**

www.innerchildpress.com/the-year-of-the-poet

World Healing, World Peace Foundation
human beings for humanity

worldhealingworldpeacefoundation.org

Ralph Bunche
1950

Each month for the year of 2020, which we have deemed as *The Year of Peace*, we at Inner Child Press International will be celebrating through our poetry a few Nobel Peace Prize Recipients who have contributed greatly to humanity via their particular avocations. This month of May 2020 you will find select poems from each Poetry Posse member on this month's celebrants.

In 1950, The Nobel Peace Prize was awarded to Ralph Bunche.

For more information about visit :

https://en.wikipedia.org/wiki/Ralph_Bunche
or
www.nobelprize.org/prizes/peace/1950/bunche/facts/

Poets . . .
sowing seeds in the
Conscious Garden of Life,
that those who have yet to come
may enjoy the Flowers.

Poets, Writers . . . know that we are the enchanting magicians that nourishes the seeds of dreams and thoughts . . . it is our words that entice the hearts and minds of others to believe there is something grand about the possibilities that life has to offer and our words tease it forth into action . . . for you are the Poet, the Writer to whom the Gift of Words has been entrusted . . .

~ wsp

poetry is . . .

Poetry succeeds where instruction fails.

~ wsp

I Fly because ...said the Dreamer to the world. I Can

www.terryunbridll.com

Gail Weston Shazor

Gail Weston Shazor

This is a creative promise ~ my pen will speak to and for the world. Enamored with letters and respectful of their power, I have been writing for most of my life. A mother, daughter, sister and grandmother I give what I have been given, greatfilledly.

Author of . . .

"An Overstanding of an Imperfect Love"
&
Notes from the Blue Roof

Lies My Grandfathers Told Me

available at Inner Child Press.

www.facebook.com/gailwestonshazor
www.innerchildpress.com/gail-weston-shazor
navypoet1@gmail.com

Collateral Damage

We studied Ralph Bunche in school
But only in February
Because we thought
Only the good blacks were born in February
And so we studied up on Ralph Bunche
And Martin Luther King and
Sojourner Truth and
Mathew Henson and
No one told us that
They had to fight to get noticed so
This light skinned man was given
The sand filled shoes Bernadotte had worn
And he marched himself east
As the next collateral damage
But little did the world know
That February born people of color
Are the most special people
Under the sun…
And like all Februarians
They changed the world.

Warrior

I got that red woman
Hid on the inside of me
We take turns hanging out
In the streets
And she balances out my navy well
When I wake after a long nite
Of perfecting your movements
She lingers across the pillow
In a preening manner
Shining the Teflon coated places
She has this repetitive way
Of telling testosterone lies
And some find her offensive
Though my sweet smile
Softens the marks cut in backs
We are much better sheathed
And while bone and sinew
Are often visible
It is only the soft kiss of lips
That you will remember
Long after you realize
You didn't get a name

Funeral

"Standing close enough to kiss, we almost touch and
pretend"
that we really didn't want to despite the yearning in our
hands;
for the closeness of the familial feel of fingers on face
my own wrapped around cheeks holding you still

while wiping a smudge off your chubby cheeks. Just a
mirror of my mothers, smiling in crooked disgust
at being tended to with a gentle assurance that just as
quickly, I might let you go before you are ready to leave.

I straighten the collar of your white shirt and smooth the
shoulders of the black suit, brushing off the invisible dust
That keeps my hands connected to you. My heart tied to the
strings that I braided with the third cord I suddenly found

dangling from the umbilical apron ties that my mother
left on the hospital bed before she departed for home.

Alicja Maria Kuberska

Alicja Maria Kuberska – awarded Polish poetess, novelist, journalist, editor. She was born in 1960, in Świebodzin, Poland. She now lives in Inowrocław, Poland.

In 2011 she published her first volume of poems entitled: "The Glass Reality". Her second volume "Analysis of Feelings", was published in 2012. The third collection "Moments" was published in English in 2014, both in Poland and in the USA. In 2014, she also published the novel - "Virtual roses" and volume of poems "On the border of dream". Next year her volume entitled "Girl in the Mirror" was published in the UK and "Love me" , " (Not)my poem" in the USA. In 2015 she also edited anthology entitled "The Other Side of the Screen".

In 2016 she edited two volumes: "Taste of Love" (USA), "Thief of Dreams" (Poland) and international anthology entitled " Love is like Air" (USA). In 2017 she published volume entitled "View from the window" (Poland). She also edits series of anthologies entitled "Metaphor of Contemporary" (Poland)

Her poems have been published in numerous anthologies and magazines in Poland, the USA, the UK, Albania, Belgium, Chile, Spain, Israel, Canada, India, Italy, Uzbekistan, Czech Republic, South Korea and Australia. She was a featured poet of New Mirage Journal (USA) in the summer of 2011.

Alicja Kuberska is a member of the Polish Writers Associations in Warsaw, Poland and IWA Bogdani, Albania. She is also a member of directors' board of Soflay Literature Foundation.

Boy with wings

Poem dedicated to Ralph Bunche

A black boy in the city of angels
hid under Grandma Lucy's wings
He quickly learned the taste of bitter childhood
And the painful touch of the angel of death

Ambition and talent gave him wings
And he rose to unattainable heights
He first crossed the invisible barrier
And he entered proudly into the world of whites

He replaced bravely the Swedish aristocrat
When he arrived in Rhodes like an angel of peace.
He brought an olive branch to the island,
To announce the Israeli-Palestinian armistice.

Epidemic

The virus stopped the world.
Time passed forward,
It looped reality.

All the doors slammed shut.
The gates of hell opened.
Death painted
Horror in the human's eyes.
It covered all faces with masks.

A new era has begun.
Nothing will be as it used to be.
Will man to man be
enemy or brother?

2020

The sky cracked.
The rider of Apocalypse
set out to the Earth.
Horse hooves crumbled
human pride and insolence.

Terrified people
locked themselves in their homes.
There are no fingerprints
on shopping carts
Smiles on their faces
are hidden under the masks.

Old values are gone.
For power, beauty and money
one can't get oxygen.
The idea of humanitarianism
broke down,
when lacked the respirators.

Invisible enemy
is lurking in the breath,
in the touch of hand.
It hides in tears.
Kisses and touches
are deadly weapons.
During the epidemic
act of supreme love
is not visiting
old parents.

Jackie Davis Allen

Jackie Davis Allen

Jackie Davis Allen, otherwise known as Jacqueline D. Allen or Jackie Allen, grew up in the Cumberland Mountains of Appalachia. As the next eldest daughter of a coal miner father and a stay at home mother, she was the first in her family to attend and graduate from college. Her siblings, in their own right, are accomplished, though she is the only one, to date, that has discovered the gift of writing.

Graduating from Radford University, with a Bachelors of Science degree in Early Education, she taught in both public and private schools. For over a decade she taught private art classes to children both in her home and at a local Art and Framing Shop where she also sold her original soft sculptured Victorian dolls and original christening gowns.

She resides in northern Virginia with her husband, taking much needed get-aways to their mountain home near the Blue Ridge Mountains, a place that evokes memories of days spent growing up in the Appalachian Mountains.

A lover of hats, she has worn many. Following marriage to her college sweetheart, and as wife, mother, grandmother, teacher, tutor, artist, writer, poet and crafter, she is a lover of art and antiques, surrounding herself, always, with books, seeking to learn more.

In 2015 she authored *Looking for Rainbows, Poetry, Prose and Art*, and in 2017, *Dark Side of the Moon*. Both books of mostly narrative poetry were published by Inner Child Press and were edited by hulya n. yilmaz.

in 2019, No Illusions.Through the Looking Glass, which was nominated to be considered for a Pulitzer Prize by the publisher and editor of InnerChild Press, ltd.

http://www.innerchildpress.com/jackie-davis-allen.php
jackiedavisallen.com

Ralph Bunche, 1904-1971:
Who Was This Man?

High School, Senior Class valedictorian.
A brilliant student and debater.
Graduate of the University of California,
Summa cum laude. And valedictorian.

A Master's and a Doctorate he earned,
In political science, from Harvard University.
While teaching at Howard University.
So, who was this man?

Perhaps, a member of the elite estate?
Blue blood of an aristocratic family?
A Roosevelt? A Rockefeller? A Kennedy?
An author? Nobel Peace Prize recipient?

He was an African American, who
By the age of thirteen had been uprooted
From his Detroit, Michigan home, to Ohio.
Then Michigan. Then New Mexico.

Absentee father. At 13, his mother's death.
Three months later, an uncle's suicide.
Whisked off, by an aunt, he and his sister. To California.
Away from their grandmother.

In 1948, Ralph Bunche, at 44, negotiated
An armistice between Egypt and Israel,
Received, in 1950, the Nobel Peace Prize.
The first ever African American to do so.

By education's ladder, in part from intelligence,
Persistence, perseverance, he climbed over obstacles
Others may have succumbed to.
So, who was this man?

African American, son of a barber,
And amateur musician mother. Ralph Bunche.
Genius of a man. Remembered
For far more than his 1950 Nobel Peace Prize.

Wings of a Butterfly

To hold you next to me
Is to love you
And to love you
Is to know you better
But, to hold a wild
And passionate body
And never
Loosen one's grip
Would be like
Tearing
Off the wings
Of a butterfly

That Which Remains

There was an old man, lived he by the sea,
Ruff, tough and gruff, so difficult to please.
With eyes ever so wary, like those of a cat...

He hesitated, yet came round where I sat.

We watched as big ships sailed in and back out.
He talked of fishing and of what little clout
He had now that he was withered and old.

Bragged a little, he once mined for gold.

Gulls gathered on the shore, needing to feed.
We fed them... fed until we filled their greed.
With courage I placed my little hand on his hand.

Avoiding my eyes, he looked down at the sand.

Ah! The fading book of time.. how it streams.
I have forgotten so much, perhaps it was a dream?
Was he my father or someone else's Dad?

Why can't I remember the last things we said?

Jackie Davis Allen

Tzemin
Ition
Tsai

Dr. Tzemin Ition Tsai (蔡澤民博士) was born in Republic of China, in 1957. He holds a Ph.D. in Chemical Engineering and two Masters of Science in Applied Mathematics and Chemical Engineering. He is a professor at Asia University (Taiwan), editor of "Reading, Writing and Teaching" academic text. He also writes the long-term columns for Chinese Language Monthly in Taiwan.

He is a scholar with a wide range of expertise, while maintaining a common and positive interest in science, engineering and literature member. He is also an editor of "Reading, Writing and Teaching" academic text and a columnist for 'Chinese Language Monthly' in Taiwan

He has won many national literary awards. His literary works have been anthologized and published in books, journals, and newspapers in more than 40 countries and have been translated into more than a dozen languages.

An Orchid Standing on the Peak

This will make me feel ashamed
If skin color becomes an issue again
At any time in the future

I am no longer surprised
If someone mentions it again
Inter-ethnic conflict and disagreement
Only reminds me of this sentence
This bridge will not no weaker and no stronger than we the
people make it

With a humble smile
He was forgotten in the world that should not be forgotten
and
We could do anything that anybody else could do

I tried to pursue his thinking which belongs to a completely
unfamiliar person
In a rational process
Decolonization for the United Nations Charter
The Universal Declaration of Human Rights
Maybe a statement closer to the truth
Although the difference between Eastern and Western
cultures, once make me surprised and overwhelmed
He has established a firm foothold in the anti-oppression
movement around the world

There are no words available to me to express the sorrow I
experience
A turbulent experience has brought peace

He was always mediating
Under the muzzles of some mutinous and very excited
soldiers
Except shouting
We must contribute to the solution of a problem on our
own doorstep
Is it possible to write a conclusion calmly?
Ralph Bunch: the soul of peace

Wind, You Have To Fly Smoothly

Oh! When the sun hovering over hillside
Wind shaking the tree shadow
How to up to you
Just do not say want to go together

Oh! Red flower opened in full on the hillside
White Butterfly Dream youth everywhere
When the wind blows smeared red lipstick
Do not only care about keen on pleasing
Forgot patrol the fields

Oh! The former hill can't compare with the back hill
So beautiful
Always secretly waiting
Must not be
Recall with nostalgia halfway water
Wind, you have to fly smoothly

The Swallows' Homeward Journey

Sunset leaves some weak light
Sky is getting dark
Elongation in the windowsill of my neck
An empty corridor
In classrooms
Was not supposed to empty
Unexpectedly dozens of vacancies
Words on the blackboard deep and shallow
This letter did not address
Where to Send
Come on sunset, remind the swallows,
Do not forget homing

Azalea trails having a partner
Duck in Surface of the lake Mullard swimming
Wave ripples continually
Reflected outside the classroom
Full of spring in the air
So comfortable, Travel in the nature landscapes
The old man nest in the classroom
Do have not ever Young?
Don't regret not having taking advantage of Young
Try a taste of skipped class
Who is going to invite the old man leaving the nest

Swallow return or no return always focus on the emotions
Youth may allow you to run wild
My heart is not old but also can understand
Eventually the semester must end
The only worry is
Belated swallow accustomed to the wild
At the final exam, do not say to me,
The topic in the paper
Reads just like hieroglyphics

Shareef Abdur Rasheed

Shareef Abdur Rasheed

Shareef Abdur-Rasheed, AKA Zakir Flo was born and raised in Brooklyn, New York. His education includes Brooklyn College, Suffolk County Community College and Makkah, Saudi Arabia. He is a Veteran of the Viet Nam era, where in 1969 he reverted to his now reverently embraced Islamic Faith. He is very active in the Islamic community and beyond with his teachings, activism and his humanity.

Shareef's spiritual expression comes through the persona of "Zakir Flo" . Zakir is Arabic for "To remind". Never silent, Shareef Abdur-Rasheed is always dropping science, love, consciousness and signs of the time in rhyme.

Shareef is the Patriarch of the Abdur-Rasheed Family with 9 Children (6 Sons and 3 Daughters) and 41 Grandchildren (24 Boys and 17 Girls).

For more information about Shareef, visit his personal FaceBook Page at :

https://www.facebook.com/shareef.abdurrasheed1
https://zakirflo.wordpress.com

Mr. Bunche

----

blossomed
stretched towards sun
proclaimed humanity one
as creator one
as earth one
as truth one
as justice one
as right one,
wrong be done
Mr. Bunche believed in peace
Mr. Bunche then received
divine commission
alleviate suspicion
demonstrate vision
mankind created by divine
intervention
to be interwoven in connection
to thee one
must be one family
he truly believed
peace, harmony
must be the reality
if we would remain
on planet like birds, fish,
plants, rain, wind,
trees, flowers
we then must stop
devouring each other
out of existence
is not an option
Mr. Bunche rose up,

Mr. Bunche spoke up,
Mr. Bunche lived on top
of the mountain
and descended
to convince humanity to
give peace a chance
Mr. Bunche danced that dance
you were blessed Mr. Bunche

food4thought = education

THINK!
----

concerning your rulers, your government
The extent of incompetence
goes through the roof
extent of lies goes through the roof
extent of crimes goes through the roof
extent of evil goes through the roof
extent of racism goes through the roof
extent of abuse of power goes through the roof
extent of theft goes through the roof
extent of arrogance goes through the roof
extent of collusion in crimes committed goes
through the roof
for instance, cold blooded murder and neglect
of the people goes through the roof
extent of more than mentioned goes through
the roof
this is the reality today in AmeriKKKa
the people have been meek in the face of tyranny
the leaders selling the country to the highest bidder
but this is not without context
to a deeeep troubled dark history
a history steeped in all the above and much more
you call this great based on the material success
of the few real capitalist that possess the capital
to benefit from capitalism?
because the vast majority in AmeriKKKa don't benefit
from that system a system that sets the table inherently
for greed, corruption, lies, murder, theft and the like
that is not in reality great that is in reality evil, wicked,
exploitative, ungodly, hypocrisy personified
the creator has warned in effect he gives lots of rope
before he tightens the noose

but when he tightens that noose no one can break loose
not all the kingdoms of the earth collectively
absolutely all power and strength belong to Allah*(swt)
thee lord of the worlds.
wait and see if you don't believe
you already saw how quick in a how your life
as you knew it flipped in a blink
remember it is written " The people get the rulers
they deserve " look at your hands and....THINK!

food4thought = education

yes
-----

these are times foretold
in real-time unfold
it's time to behold
it's now to be whole
yo do ya'll know?
you who was fashioned
created made into a congealed
clot in the womb a soul getting
made in a boat a float
in the dark without breathing
without lungs filled until the
moment is here to fill up on air
at any time, the maker can stop
degree it's over by saying ' be '
but at his command you complete
the process
coming out to the other side a success
but yet you stand out as an open
adversary as though you made yourself
the vast majority have turned your backs
on the giver of life, death
who said he and you was?
yet you refuse to adhere to the rules
put here
it's in you or not
manifest by the god fear
knowing to do what he says is the only way
no, no, you refused to submit
following the whispers fake tip from him
who whispered into the heart?
lead you astray on a dead-end trip
because you didn't obey the warning

stay away obey me now
you can't obey him who's a
enemy avowed but some how
you were yawning
thus, here we are at this hour getting
a dose of his power
that there is no power or strength
but Allah*(swt)
you once again are given pause to
ponder pray tell
as death lurks in position to pounce
and take every ounce of your soul
a bacterium or whatever is not what
delivers death's blow
it's Allah only who knows the hour
he has written for us all to go
return back from hence we come
now or later it's promised to be our
turn
know this and learn
from Allah we come and back to him
is our return

food4thought = education

*(swt) = All glory to Allah.

Kimberly Burnham

Kimberly Burnham

A brain health expert with a PhD in Integrative Medicine, Kimberly Burnham has lived in tropical Colombia; in Belgium during the Vietnam War; in Japan teaching businessmen English; in diverse international Toronto, Canada and several places in the US. Now, she's in Spokane, WA with her wife, Elizabeth, two sets of twins (age 11 & 14) and three dogs. Her recent book, *Awakenings: Peace Dictionary, Language and the Mind, a Daily Brain Health Program* includes the word for peace in hundreds of languages. Kim's poetry weaves through 70 volumes of *The Year of the Poet, Inspired by Gandhi, Women Building the World, A Woman's Place in the Dictionary*, Tiferet Journal, Human/Kind Journal and more.

https://www.nervewhisperer.solutions/
https://www.linkedin.com/in/kimberlyburnham/

Cease-Fire Follows Tumultuous Birth

At the tumultuous birth
among murder and mayhem
in 1948 the state of Israel came to be
helped on the journey
by the hand of the first African American
awarded the Nobel Peace Prize
he soothed the way
a cease-fire between Israelis and Arabs
Shalom Salaam Peace
"There are no warlike people
just warlike leaders"
said Ralph Bunche
after tough negotiations

SLM

The differences are nuanced and pronounced between
the Muslim world and the Jewish world
between Arabic and Hebrew
finding peace Salaam سلام and Shalom שלום
in common three consonants S-L-M
yes the writing is different
but the Semitic roots are the same
the cultures may not find peace
but look how vastly different worlds say
this word of comfort, of prosperity
wholeness and health
what brings peace is not the same
for any two people
not the identical for any two cultures
but look how much is similar
"Shalom" in Hebrew of Israel
"Salaam" in Arabic of the Middle East
"Salaamata" in Afar of Ethiopia
"Salum" in Bukharic of Central Asia
"Sala" in Balochi of Iran
"Saljám" made it into Russian
a loan word from Muslims and Jews
written салям in Cyrillic letters
"Selum" in Jibbali Geblet of South Arabia
"Šlm" in Ugaritic of Syria
and "Sholem" in Yiddish of Israel

Ch'ewata Talking in Peace

As in most cultures in Ethiopia
the Kafa sit together
talking in peace
"Salamoona"
this is the essence of life
relationships are strengthened
constantly updated by greetings
visits, drinking coffee and eating together
the preparation of food and beverages is important
but talking together ጨዋታ "ch'ewata"
from the verb to play
is the heart of life

Elizabeth E. Castillo

Elizabeth Esguerra Castillo is a multi-awarded and an Internationally-Published Contemporary Author/Poet and a Professional Writer / Creative Writer / Feature Writer / Journalist / Travel Writer from the Philippines. She has 2 published books, "Seasons of Emotions" (UK) and "Inner Reflections of the Muse", (USA). Elizabeth is also a co-author to more than 60 international anthologies in the USA, Canada, UK, Romania, India. She is a Contributing Editor of Inner Child Magazine, USA and an Advisory Board Member of Reflection Magazine, an international literary magazine. She is a member of the American Authors Association (AAA) and PEN International.

Web links:

Facebook Fan Page

https://free.facebook.com/ElizabethEsguerraCastillo

Google Plus

https://plus.google.com/u/0/+ElizabethCastillo

Bunche, American Odyssey

Here was a titan of 20th century diplomacy,

Coined as an American Odyssey

1940s, led Israel's mediation,

Did peacekeeping efforts to places in division

On to the Middle East, Africa, and Mediterranean,

And also contributed to the freedom struggle of African

American.

Ring of Light

I met you from the past,
In one of my reincarnations-
An unfinished business we must face
A broken soul must be set free
Or to be chained 'til eternity.

At the crossroads, we met once more
My soul recognizing you in an instant,
From the eddies, sparks ignited
Setting up constellations from above,
Cosmic dots intertwining our hearts.

At a certain point some place else,
The two of us seated in a carriage
To the point of no return-
A ring of light flashing before our eyes,
Blinding us for a moment.

Here, the Aleph ceases time and space
Bringing us back to where our eyes first gazed
Centuries past but the scars remain,
When will the wounds ever heal?
Redemption, liberation can we still feel?

The ring of light gives you the answers,
Even of the unspoken questions
The deafening silence between two hearts
The raging emotions burning from inside,
Casting a mystic spell, setting you free.

Transition

We are on an energy shift,
As the sun is on a transition,
The "corona" symbolizing
A new order, a new world.

Cast out fear and worry,
Meditate and cleanse the soul
We are in for a new beginning,
A new Earth is dawning.

Mother Nature is healing,
Years of destruction cleansed
She's preparing an Eternal Home,
To get back to Paradiso.

Joe
Paire

Joe Paire

Joseph L Paire' aka Joe DaVerbal Minddancer . . .
is a quiet man, born in a time where civil liberties
were a walk on thin ice. He's been a victim of his
own shyness often sidelined in his own quest for
love. He became the observer, charting life's path.
Taking note of the why, people do what they do. His
writings oft times strike a cord with the
dormant strings of the reader. His pen the rosined
bow drawn across the mind. He comes full-frontal
or in the subtlest way, always expressing in a way
that stimulate the senses.

www.facebook.com/joe.minddancer

The Struggle of Color

Was there ever a time when men were accepted
were they highly respected, while we reflect on this man
Ralph Johnson Bunche
Nobel Peace Prize, summa cum laude, Phi Beta Kappa.
Now I ask you, was there ever a time
We can do all the right things
When we all do the right things
The difference is not our distances
It is the resistance to our differences
The difference is our hue
Surprisingly, our view is as diverse as the universe
We are cursed with some perverse ideas
that beyond this sphere
There is a place that will erase that perception
a little deflection from the man at hand
Ralph Johnson Bunche
the list of his accomplishments in a time when
that time was less disguised,
The flags of the United Nations fly
The march on Washington
Selma to Montgomery
Voting Rights Act of 1965
Was there ever a time when the color of a mother's son
was there ever a time when another mothers son
Was run out on a rail, or nailed, or jailed
or roped into a symbol of inequity
A six dollar figure could never be a
you look taller than I thought
The shade of suspicion taught
I thought I'd ought to look a little deeper
      Ralph Johnson Bunche
Nobel Peace Keeper.

Stay at Home Person

Has education taken a turn for the worse?
I think not my friends
Have you noticed what you haven't noticed in years?
Of course, you have, unless you're essential
Have you had to leave your rental?
Your mental is on borrowed time
How you sense the world has been amplified
you wonder why you wander
"I want to go outside in the rain"
Doesn't seem funny now, that little song refrain
or sayings like "stop and smell the roses"
in our covered noses
Outside poses, "The Who" knows this
"See me, Feel me",
as we struggle with being alone this way
This way of my way
This why me, this why we as a people
This how we so simple to follow the pie man
Why Man?
cover your nose and wash your hands.

Stimulus Package

If I could run a racket, with all the frills
I would probably be employed near capitol hill
Suit and tie, cufflinked shirts
looking high and mighty and dealing in dirt
No taxes to pay, well not from my pocket
I bought a Judge, so I am never on the docket
my cronies are in lock step
my enemies are on the watch list
now watch this space, I have the media laced
Why groupies woo me with idiotic polices
Now the sheep that follow me,
deep down, are a part of me
family seed know no bounds
Release the hounds
so, lets distribute this money funny
this funny money, these ill-gotten gains from caused pain
make it rain for the reign I spelled Reich wrong
this may seem a might strong but its easy money
when we ease this money back into the economy
Back to the CEO-NOMY mmm. Co-money?
Either way this stimulates my package if you get my drift
The gist is this, its all about the exchange of funds
To be estranged from funds is beneath this job
If I could run a racket, with all the frills
I would probably be employed near capitol hill
Suit and tie, cufflinked shirts
looking high and mighty and dealing in dirt

hülya

n.

yılmaz

Liberal Arts Emerita, hülya n. yılmaz is a published author, literary translator, and Co-Chair and Director of Editing Services at Inner Child Press International. Her poetic work appeared in an excess of eighty-five anthologies of global endeavors and has been presented at numerous national and international poetry events. In 2018, the Writer's International Network of British Colombia, Canada honored yılmaz with a literary award. As of 2017, two of her poems remain permanently installed in *Telepoem Booth* – a U.S.-wide poetic art exhibition. hülya finds it vital for everyone to understand a deeper sense of self, and writes creatively to attain a comprehensive awareness for and development of our humanity.

Writing Web Site
https://hulyanyilmaz.com/

Editing Web Site
https://hulyasfreelancing.com

What's on My Mind?

It is no easy feat to hope for a future.
A deadly virus is spreading fast,
Reigning over the world these days.

Eagerness of the recent past to talk about peace
Seems to have seized to be. At least for me.
Not much to expect for the mortals.

So, I am letting my demons out to play today.
While they are having the time of their lives,
I delve into my imaginary space.

I seek an answer for my concerns from Ralph Bunche,
The first African American to be singled out
With the honor of a Nobel's Peace Prize.

One source says that his father, a barber,
Had a clientele of whites only.
Easy to picture what he must have gone through.

The son's peaceful initiatives, though, prevailed.
He most certainly had his objectives intact.
Even in our dark times, we hail his success.

Also 2020 insists on discriminating against our co-souls,
Even when the fatal danger is the one and the same.
Too many people are still ignorant, seeing it all as a game.

White men's risky cures for this century's chief-virus
Are being tested on our black sisters and brothers.
Once again, segregationist agendas smother them lethally.

I know, my poem does not do this great man any justice,
As there is much with which to fill in the blanks.
You as well as I know, we now have a noble task at hand.

The 1950 Nobel Peace Prize

setting up world peace

1949 Armistice Agreements

in the Middle East

Martin Luther King's Influence

integrationist

the first person of color

a legend's imprint

Teresa E. Gallion

Teresa E. Gallion was born in Shreveport, Louisiana and moved to Illinois at the age of 15. She completed her undergraduate training at the University of Illinois Chicago and received her master's degree in Psychology from Bowling Green State University in Ohio. She retired from New Mexico state government in 2012.

She moved to New Mexico in 1987. While writing sporadically for many years, in 1998 she started reading her work in the local Albuquerque poetry community. She has been a featured reader at local coffee houses, bookstores, art galleries, museums, libraries, Outpost Performance Space, the Route 66 Festival in 2001 and the State of Oklahoma's Poetry Festival in Cheyenne, Oklahoma in 2004. She occasionally hosts an open mic.

Teresa's work is published in numerous Journals and anthologies. She has two CDs: *On the Wings of the Wind* and *Poems from Chasing Light*. She has published three books: *Walking Sacred Ground, Contemplation in the High Desert* and *Chasing Light.*

Chasing Light was a finalist in the 2013 New Mexico/Arizona Book Awards.

The surreal high desert landscape and her personal spiritual journey influence the writing of this Albuquerque poet. When she is not writing, she is committed to hiking the enchanted landscapes of New Mexico. You may preview her work at

http://bit.ly/1aIVPNq or *http://bit.ly/13IMLGh*

American Nobel Peace Laureate

Ralph Johnson Bunche, man of color
political scientist, academic, diplomat
honored for brokering peace between
Israel and Egypt.

Involved in the formation of the United Nations,
a major role player in its peacekeeping
initiatives 1945 to 1971. A respected negotiator
for peace in the Middle East and Africa.

Bunche was an active supporter of
the Civil Rights Movement in the United States.
He participated in the 1963 March on Washington,
the Selma to Montgomery, Alabama march in 1965
and vocally confronted racial discrimination in his home
in Queens, New York and across the United States,

Together We Can

There is a place inside you and me
where peace resides.
I know.
I have been there.

That's why my smile sings
even on my down days.
Because I know,
we can make it there again.

Let's just sing and dance
today to honor the blue sky
and the green grass
bending in the meadow.

Tomorrow waits with patience
for those with courage
to move beyond violence
to the trail of compassion.

Go Get Fat

There is bread on the mountain
for hungry souls.
Fed through the third eye,

you risk getting fat
on beauty infusions
wandering on a trail.

Soaring peaks, evergreen forest
succulent waterfalls, wild rivers
and peaceful lakes feed the soul.

What are you waiting for?
Go for a buffet of grandeur.
The mountain waits to greet you.

Ashok
K.
Bhargava

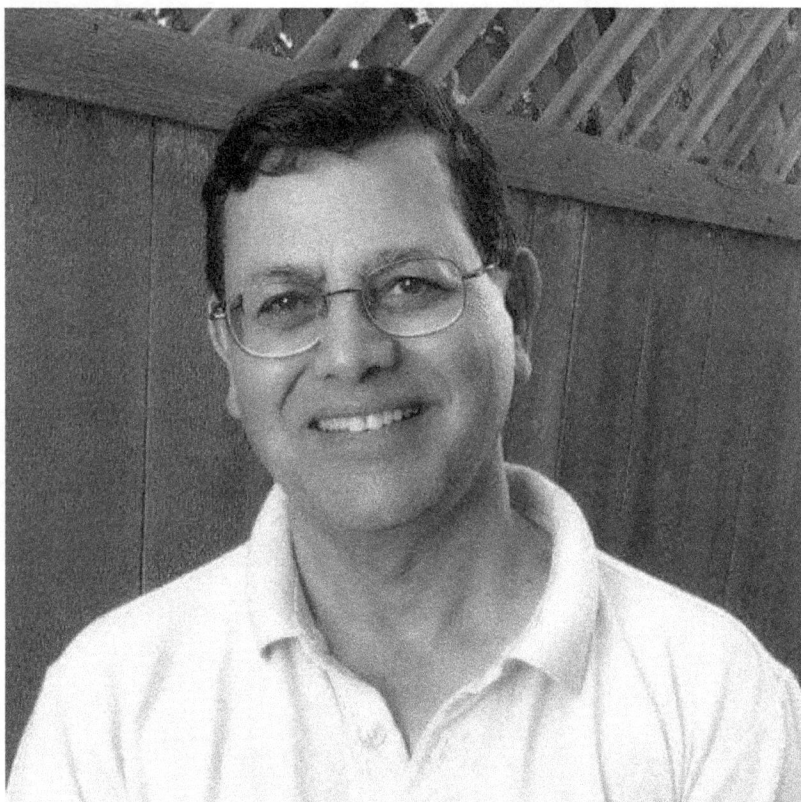

Ashok Bhargava is a poet, writer, community activist, public speaker, management consultant and a keen photographer. Based in Vancouver, he has published several collections of his poems: Riding the Tide, Mirror of Dreams, A Kernel of Truth, Skipping Stones, Half Open Door and Lost in the Morning Calm. His poetry has been published in various literary magazines and anthologies.

Ashok is a Poet Laureate and poet ambassador to Japan, Korea and India. He is founder of WIN: Writers International Network Canada. Its main objective is to inspire, encourage, promote and recognize writers of diverse genres, artists and community leaders. He has received many accolades including Nehru Humanitarian Award for his leadership of Writers International Network Canada, Poets without Borders Peace Award for his journeys across the globe to celebrate peace and to create alliances with poets, and Kalidasa Award for creative writings.

What an Irony

I sit to write a poem about peace
my thoughts return to why
we take it for granted

that a man named Trump
in charge of bombs
with no backbone

on golf course he talks about fire and fury,
he tweets at 3:00 at night that
he has a bigger nuclear button than North Korea

he does not know Ralph Bunche
neither does he care, oddly
he is President of America

Nothing Forgotten

Lawns wet from rain in the night
Birds settled over powerlines
People inside in homes
Streets deserted

No good news for weeks
Announcements and warnings
Lockdowns
Social distancing
Stay indoors
Wash hands

I remember you
Hands clasped
Forehead bowed
How you accepted and
looked beyond

You prayed for another chance
A new beginning

Be together with others
Eat, sing, dance, endure
Sleep, wakeup for morning walk

But it was the end
No more breath
Only silence

Nothing forgotten
Nothing overlooked

You left
Quietly
Without
Any uncertainty

In This Next Moment I Will…

start a new day
        a new dream
and walk into what I am
                an image of a giant bird
made of clouds
                in the skies.
I will wander   explore
mountains, forests, rivers, seas
                and barren cities
                        locked down   so what.
Here I am not alone
I am with the hopes, feelings and anxieties
                held in layers
                        tightly woven together.
Each moment
                new each time
                        eternally   whatever
happens   happens
yet we'll make it
through   Coronavirus
        journey through it
                together.

Ashok K. Bhargava

Caroline
'Ceri Naz'
Nazareno
Gabis

Carolin 'Ceri' Nazareno-Gabis

Caroline 'Ceri Naz' Nazareno-Gabis, World Poetry Canada International Director to Philippines is known as a 'poet of peace and friendship', a multi-awarded poet, editor, journalist, speaker, linguist, educator, peace and women's advocate. She believes that learning other's language and culture is a doorway to wisdom.

Among her poetic belts include 7 th Prize Winner in the 19 th and 20 th Italian Award of Literary Festival; Writers International Network-Canada "Amazing Poet 2015", The Frang Bardhi Literary Prize 2014 (Albania), the sair-gazeteci or Poet Journalist Award 2014 (Tuzla, Istanbul, Turkey) and World Poetry Empowered Poet 2013 (Vancouver, Canada). She's a featured member of Association of Women's Rights and Development (AWID), The Poetry Posse, Galaktika Poetike, Asia Pacific Writers and Translators (APWT), Axlepino and Anacbanua.

Her poetry and children's stories have been featured in different anthologies and magazines worldwide.

Links to her works:

panitikan.ph/2018/03/30/caroline-nazareno-gabis
apwriters.org/author/ceri_naz
www.aveviajera.org/nacionesunidasdelasletras/id1181
.html

Bunche World View of Race

Thinking big to march against slavery

He delivered the rights of the Negros in America

With Martin Luther, he built no fear

His influence through speeches

That racial discrimination is not a reason

To separate the blacks from whites,

Thus, democracy is color blind!

Bunche, your phenomenal milestone

Brought pride to the Black History

Your ideas become the spirit of hopefulness

Your belief that everyone should progress

Without racism isn't an illusion

It was a big dream conquered

In the name of peace.

fly like a butterfly...

your propelled wings

show how to blossom

courage to face new beginnings,

even some days

don't agree with the weather

you're expecting...

what matters is

you become a beautiful butterfly

flying free

bringing sunny days

though your eyes

are keeping rainy days

ode to a portrait

the pen and ink
marrying the canvas
is the passion you convey
the best sketch
you're framing is yourself
the best colours running through your hands
are the symphonies of your humble heart,
the best image being treasured
is your beautiful soul
the best photo of the day
reflects your goodwill
your great self as a whole
the force beyond four corners
beyond the portrait without borders.

Swapna Behera

Swapna Behera is a bilingual contemporary poet, author, translator and editor from Odisha, India. She was a teacher from 1984 to 2015. Her stories, poems and articles are widely published in National and International journals, and ezines, and are translated into different national and International languages. She has penned six books. She is the recipient of the Prestigious International Mother Language UGADI AWARD WINNER 2019. She was conferred upon the Prestigious International Poesis Award of Honor at the 2nd Bharat Award for Literature as Jury in 2015, The Enchanting Muse Award in India World Poetree Festival 2017, World Icon of Peace Award in 2017, and the Pentasi B World Fellow Poet in 2017. She is the recipient of Gold Cross of Wisdom Award, the Prolific Poetess Award, The Life time Achievement Award, The Best Planner Award, The Sahitya Shiromani Award, ATAL BIHARI BAJPAYEE AWARD 2018, Ambassador De Literature Award 2018, Global Literature Guardian Award, International Life Time Achievement Award and the Master of Creative Impulse Award. She has received the Honoured Poet of India from the Seychelles Government accredited Literary Society LLSF. Her one poem A NIGHT IN THE REFUGEE CAMP is translated into 50 languages. She is the Ambassador of Humanity by Hafrikan Prince Art World Africa 2018 and an official member of World Nation's Writers Union, Kazakhstan 2018. Italy, the National President for India by Hispanomundial Union of Writers (UHE), Peru, the administrator of several poetic groups, and the Cultural Ambassador for India and south Asia of Inner Child Press U.S.

sincerely yours ....

the catastrophic cloud represents
a city
that stands in the distant land or in my heart
strangers have no voice
they just rearrange the dreams
make the sand dunes and oasis

the digital footmarks on the time zones
only frame a number ,a code
neither I nor you have any promises for the ether
death is a bureaucrat
it can arrive from nowhere to every where

there is hunger
preserved in every cold stomach
no churning ,no smell of spices
no fluttering
dead butterfly wings can never explain colours
everything can start fresh
concealed lips will open
windows will throw glances
listening will do a magic
shapes of solitude will profuse
already jasmines bloom in the abandoned courtyards
to recreate
a bridge ,a play ground ,a school
grand mothers are still on the road march
planting basils to sanitise each house
the ground zero workers
are
building the city in a do or die mode
because
they are sincerely yours
indeed sincerely yours

the lost key of a palace

the mirror house reflects
 grass ,clouds and an image
that is as orphan as the intestines
on the post mortem table.

while crossing the main road
the garish dialogues frame Mona Lisa smile
everything seems so organised
yet
the virgin eyes seek pure love
the hymn of life is flashed
on the beaks of the parrots

the strange oxymoron
searching the lost key of palace
without any price tag..........of lost democracy !!

Swapna Behera

a mediator's clarion call .....

the first African American
a political scientist
Ralph Johnson Bunche
son of a barber and musician
gets the scholarship from Harvard University
studies the colonial policy in West Africa
active in civil rights movements
a service that he rendered for United Nations
a mediator and peace negotiator in Middle East
 arranged the cease fire
 between Israelis and Arabs

certainly an arduous task
to divide Palestine between Arabs and Jews

the Arabs rejected the resolutions of United Nations
 concerning Jewish state
"people never like wars
leaders like wars'' said he

eleven months of negotiations
concluded with the armistice agreements
"If you want to get across an idea, wrap it up in a person''
 clarion call for tenacity and persistence
no room for bigotry in democracy
that's why he received Noble Peace Prize
he   a peace maker and mentor
we remember you dear professor .....

Albert 'Infinite' Carrasco

Albert "Infinite The Poet" Carrasco is an urban poet, mentor and public speaker.

Albert believes his experience of growing up in poverty, dealing with drugs and witnessing murder over and over were lessons learnt, in order to gain knowledge to teach. Albert's harsh reality and honesty is a powerfully packed punch delivered through rhyme. Infinite grew up in the east part of the Bronx and still resides there, so he knows many young men will follow the same dark path he followed looking for change. The life of crime should never be an option to being poor but it is, very often.

Infinite poetry @lulu.com

Alcarrasco2 on YouTube

Infinite the poet on reverbnation

Infinite Poetry

http://www.lulu.com/us/en/shop/al-infinite-carrasco/infinite-poetry/paperback/product-21040240.html

Ralph Johnson Bunche

In 1904 Ralph Johnson Bunche was born in Detroit
Michigan,
His father was a barber and his mother was an amateur
musician.
his grandmother was born into slavery.
When Ralph Johnson Bunche was ten years old he moved
to Albuquerque,
Two years later his parents died,
Him and his two sisters were lucky,
they had a strong grandmother that took good care of the
branches of the family tree.
They moved to Los Angeles.
Ralph started working to help with finances.
He was very intelligent.
He was valedictorian in elementary,
Got a scholarship to Harvard and earned his master's
degree,
Then started teaching in Howard university,
While he continued to go to Harvard for his doctorate
degree.
Bunche was a teacher and student that was active in the
civil rights movement.
His fame will arise from his service to the us government.
He did and achieved so many things, too many to mention,
Ralph Johnson Bunche became the first African American
to receive the Nobel peace prize
For mediating Arab and Jew tension.

Corona

Waking up to deal with death,
Going to sleep remembering those that took their last
breath.
Horrific times,
Horror fills the mind.
You can't unsee what you're witnessing,
You can't undo what's done,
You're praying for the best but watching the worst
outcome.
It's amazing to see those loved filled hearts,
Man the frontline to play their part.
You guys are heroes,
Life savers,
Saviors to survivors,
Rays of hope finding ways to cope.
No monetary figure can show your worth.
You're the first responders to deal with this covid drama,
The ones to deal with covid trauma.
Most have their own children,
but their call to duty is to try to save other mothers
immaculate conceptions.

Bottom to the top

I went from the bottom to the top and always stood being a boss even when I had to come back down and get my own color off, whether it was good times or wartime my job was to keep shop open and money coming in at all cost. Inf is a protege of old reys of her-ron and yey. I never let em down, I was destined to be the heir of the throne, always aired shit out to make sure the throne was never overthrown. We was either good money or i saw you as enemy, there was no in between, no one was around me unless you was a plug, shooter or a worker on the block feeding fiends. My life was all about drugs, guns and lucrative traps in and out the slums, went to bed at night counting funds and a few minutes after waking up my pointer and thumbs went numb, kept fresh gems but no matter how sharp they were, when you chop cookies there was always crumbs. I got tired of baggn shake so I left the powder on the plate then re melted it after a while, sometimes it would be and extra twenty eight. Stood on hot blocks discreetly moving rock since taj mahaj tops, strapped with one in the top and thirty two underneath for when there's beef. infinite is a veteran, one of the last living legends, I could open up any block and shut down every opp, if I wanted to I can monopolize all over again but I retired from birds and if I start again that'll be hustln backwards, so I leveled up, now I'm hustl'n words.

Eliza Segiet

Eliza Segiet - A graduate of Jagiellonian University, The author of poetry volumes. *Romans z sobą [Romance with Oneself]* (2013), *Myślne miraże [Mental Mirages]*(2014), *Chmurność [Cloudiness]* (2016), *Magnetyczni* (2018) *Magnetic People*- translation published in The USA in 2018, *Nieparzyści [Unpaired]* (2019), A monodrama *Prześwity [Clearance]* (2015), a farce *Tandem [Tandem]* (2017), Mini novel *Bezgłośni [Voiceless]*(2019). Her poems can be found in numerous anthologies both in Poland and abroad. She is a member of The Association of Polish Writers and The World Nations Writers Union. The laureate of The International Annual Publication of 2017 for the poem Questions, and for the Sea of Mist in Spillwords Press in 2018. For her volume of Magnetic People she won a literary award of a Golden Rose named after Jaroslaw Zielinski (Poland 2019 r.). Her poem The *Sea of Mists* was chosen as one of the best amidst the hundred best poems of 2018 by International Poetry Press Publication Canada. In The 2019 Poet's Yearbook, as the author of *Sea of Mists*, she was awarded with the prestigious Elite Writer's Status Award as one of the best poets of 2019 (July 2019).

She was awarded *World Poetic Star Award* by World Nations Writers Union – the world's largest Writers' Union from Kazakhstan (August 2019).
In September 2019 she was 1st Place Laureate (Foreign Poetry category) – in Contest *Quando È la Vita ad Invitare* for poem *Be Yourself* (Italy).
Her poem *Order* from volume *Unpaired* was selected as one of the 100 best poems of 2019 in International Poetry Press Publications (Canada).
In November 2019 she is a nominee for Pushcart Prize.

Origin

To the memory of Ralph Bunche ~
Nobel Peace Prize laureate of 1950.

He was convinced that
a human is not deprived of goodness,
but should draw it from the self.

A mistake
is to divide people
by the cause of their origin.

A harmony in the world
– not just for victims of daltonism.
Those unconcerned about skin color differences
they know,
what tolerance and acceptance is.

He aimed,
for the words *peace* and *freedom*
to be
exactly,
what they mean.

Wars are not merely fights and suffering,
but also are a loss of dignity.
Everyone ought to
have the views for a new day.

– And life needs to be given a chance!

translated by Ula de B

Paradise

I filled my eyes with beauty and ugliness.
In the damp basement
I recall
the murmur of the river,
which,
without paying heed to the obstacles,
douched the still boulders.
For years, in the same place
the anchored stones
did not allow the elements
to move them elsewhere.

The relentless, mindless
figments of the earth
are to be harder than the human?

I will drift with the current of life
—I will find my paradise.

translated by Artur Komoter

Roads

The roads are not always lit,
we do not know who will come out of the corner
– a brother or an enemy.
And when both are evil?
You have to trust
that the good time,
– will remain
and will be what has to be.

Everyday life
changes one,
and words
– do not have to hurt.

translated by Artur Komoter

William S. Peters Sr.

Bill's writing career spans a period of over 50 years. Being first Published in 1972, Bill has since went on to Author in excess of 50 additional Volumes of Poetry, Short Stories, etc., expressing his thoughts on matters of the Heart, Spirit, Consciousness and Humanity. His primary focus is that of Love, Peace and Understanding!

Bill says . . .

I have always likened Life to that of a Garden. So, for me, Life is simply about the Seeds we Sow and Nourish. All things we "Think and Do", will "Be" Cause and eventually manifest itself to being an "Effect" within our own personal "Existences" and "Experiences" . . . whether it be Fruit, Flowers, Weeds or Barren Landscapes! Bill highly regards the Fruits of his Labor and wishes that everyone would thus go on to plant "Lovely" Seeds on "Good Ground" in their own Gardens of Life!

to connect with Bill, he is all things Inner Child

www.iaminnerchild.com

Personal Web Site

www.iamjustbill.com

Conviction

He witnessed far too much turmoil
Where the peace of the people
Waned into
An almost non-existence

He knew with an absolute certainty
That this was not just a [plight-blight
Of his own innate community,
But that of the global neighborhood

So . . .
He educated himself,
Taught what he learned
And what he believed
And shouted, marched
And discussed his ideas
And adopted ideologies
With other leaders
Who though perhaps
Similarly . . .

And it worked,
They listened
And the followed
The pathway he laid
To peace for all men

Ralph Bunche

Her

It was a day of Angels,
And her holy presence
Gave cause for them to sing
Sweet melodies of love
Within the recesses of my guarded heart

I wanted so desperately to dance,
But my limbs were frozen
With an awe
That comes upon me
Every time she comes unto me

Her grace was a light one
That permeated
All of my darkness

Her fragrance made the flowers
Undulate
With a mesmerizing sensuality
That I have always longed for,
And here she is,
As they are
Imparting unto my soul
A divine 'Trance'
That sweeps my being-ness
To lie prone
Before the Throne
Of creation

Most certifiably,
I am blessed,
And I live this

With a gratitude of certainty
That none may refute,
Reject,
Nor rebuke

Mere love alone
Is small
In her presence,
For she brings unto me
A greater light-filled understanding
Of who i can be,
And who 'I AM' . . .
….
Yes, it is 'Her'
My divine feminine,
My 'She-ness'
That actualizes
A beauty beyond wonder

Her !!!

My Fault

I did not have anything
To do with it! . . . hhhhmmmmm

I did not ask for you
To drop bombs
On the villages, towns and cities
Of my fellow human beings

Why are you making more bullets,
And bombs
And disease
To kill others,
My sisters, my brothers,
Whom I have never met

Politicians,
Doing the bidding
Of the 'Greed Merchants'
For oil, land
And any other resources
That belong to the Mother
And the people
Of the earth

They live in castles
With more than enough,
But they want more . . . for ?

They look out their guarded windows
And they see possibilities
Of greed . . .
They see the sunshine of growth

I look out the blood-stained glass
Of my window,
And I see fear,
Death,
And more fear
That we will not make it
As a humanity
As long as we continue
Our silence
And allow the demons
To rule

The common 'school of thought'
These days,
Is based upon us
Attempting to make a way . . .
To live,
Feed our families,
Pay the bills
That are slowly choking us
To death

We wish to educate our children,
With truth,
Compassion,
Sincerity,
Gratitude,
Understanding,
And Love for all things . . .
But where do we find these sacred seeds
To plant in the gardens
Of their future
When there is so much blight
Upon us

Is it 'My Fault' ?
I say it is . . .
But I also say it is not,
Yet what we now have
Is what we got,
Because I did not speak,
Raise my voice in protest,
Shout loud enough
To effectuate any change,
And with that
The ugliness perpetuated itself
Upon us all . . .

Yes it is time for change !
......
And should we fail
To assail ourselves
Upon this prevailing evil . . .
Then yes . . .
It is . . . .
MY FAULT!!!!

William S. Peters, Sr.

May
2020
Featured Poets

~ * ~

Alok Kumar Ray

Eden S. Trinidad

Franco Barbato

Izabela Zubko

i Fly

because

...said the Dreamer to the world.

I Can

www.iamjustbill.com

Alok
Kumar
Ray

Dr. Ray by profession is a lecturer who teaches Political Science to both undergraduate and postgraduate students. Being a bilingual poet (Odia and English) many poems written by him have been published in many national and international anthologies, magazines, tabloids etc. He dwells at Kendrapara district headquarters in Odisha state of India.

Smile is an Asset

A smiling face we all appreciate as asset
It feels good for us to associate without any pretext

Smile with blink of an eye makes us happy
So penetrating it is that each one wants it to copy

It cools an aggrieved soul like rain does to a parched field
With smile in your face you can achieve miracles indeed

Smile of a child is so soothing and captivating
Like the morning Sun it touches all , very enchanting

A smile has the power to subdue the tempo of anger
It binds us in rapture , keeps us afresh very longer

Smile of the lover mitigates all hues and cry
Beloved is mesmerized, forgets past area so grey

A crooked smile has the capacity to turn your enemy as a
fool
You can encash enough dividends when smile acts as a tool

In silver screens we see smiling face of heroes and heroines
It takes us to a state where we feel sizzling sensation in
arteries and veins
A politician has expertise in manipulation of different
aspects of smile
We people are so engrossed that we forget everything for a
while

Repentance

I only wanted your selfless love, total dedication
Leave the past as a nightmare behind
The dullness of my life, was so painful, disgusting, stressful
, the life should rise above now
Night let filled with joy and contentment, a gentle breeze
let blow
As I proceed for a brand new life
I only wanted your bygone love, your unconditional
surrender

A defeaning uproar I hear all around
Piercing into my very heart and soul
It echoes the voice of my soul
Cinematographically all are displayed
To eyes these are gruesome

I only wanted your pure love, your blind acceptance
The curtains fell upon that scattered my dreams
In a strange manner I only witnessed to see
I preserved all those sweet memories
A piece like diamond that dazzles my eyes
Eyes succumb to rays of that light
The light so gorgeous, also moonlit like cold
Oblivion, nothing concrete is going to happen!!!

Volatile Mood

Summer is speeding up obviously in a greater pace
Quickly preparing own self to go to native place
We all are in hurry mood and are as if in a race
Mood is fluctuating, need cool breeze to energize base

Oh lo ! I have changed the plan in the meanwhile
The tour was cancelled that made me volatile
Went out for evening walk as usual in own style
Searched something important from bookrack's file

Now writing for literary groups with enthusiasm
This relieves me from monotony and shields sarcasm

Eden S. Trinidad

Eden Soriano Trinidad hails from the Philippines. She is a Lifetime Achievement Awardee on the 12th Guntur International Poetry Festival and Poetry on Wheels held in Guntur, Andra, Pradesh and Hyderabad, India September 18-23, 2019.

Her Eden Blooms, a bilingual book has been released on this occasion, translated and published by Dr. Lanka Siva Rama Prasad.

She translated in the Filipino Language an epic poetry book of Dr. L Sr Prasad, titled "The Casket of Vermillion", and Zen Poem collections of Krishna Prasai.

Every Saturday her poems are being translated, recited and aired over Internet Radio in Mexico Vision Universal Radio program in English and Spanish Languages.

Last Years, This Year

I thank the past years for all those who walked into my life
They all professed and added savor to my already flavored
full life
Gallant, romantic, poetic friendly souls
You are all dear and enthralling.

Thank God for this green planet which carries our feet,
Mingling with us the trashes, and clutters that we shredded.
Thank God last year was the future
This year is our new future.

Always be excited as our eyes flap open
While our ears and lips tingling on the "radio smiles" on
the streets
Within lies an immensurable treasure in each one of us.

Shall we smile more often, respect more often, love more
often
Share more and make more new friends
Let's all be excited, and be expectant
On tremendous blessings and life's surprises!

Our hearts would burst with joy
Let's laugh often and clap our hands often
Express freely our admiration
Mind not the negative vibration

Our hearts and spirit unruffled
Expectantly waiting for great things to unfold.

Oh, Palm!

She offered him a flower…
Her palm excites him surprisingly.
It looks too good for poetry.

He wanted to shower it with kisses
And grab it tenderly.

Her palm drives him crazy
And feel her palm is sultry.

Finds it so lovely,
And wish…their palm to marry.

The palm pine for heaven,
Touch- me not, cheeks burnt shyly.

Oh, Palm!
I want you dearly.

Gorgeous as flowers that she touches,
That she finds along life's byway.

My Only One

He fell in love with me,
For the first time …
I was sporting a navy collar top
And my hair tied up in a ponytail.
(I was 12 years old then)

He fell in love with me
On the second time,
I was chasing rainbows.
I was scaling heights of many mountains
I was persevering to attain my dreams.
 (I was 40 years old.)

He falls in love with me
In every turning of the new leaf
While I'm engrossed with my e-pen
Scribbling, writing, composing.

He is always proud of me
He prided himself
in every achievement and prestige
that I achieved every day.

My first love, my closest friend,
My faithful husband,
My number-one fan until the end.

Holding hands while we calmly
 traversed life's valleys and dales
Tossed in many roaring rivers and life's upsurges
Under the scorching heat of the sun

Turbulent, stormy and strong rains
Like the rising of the sun every morning
And the phases of the moon every evening
Our love will forever go on
Like our wedding ring which did not end
on our honeymooning.

Eden S. Trinidad

Franco Barbato

Franco Barbato

Franco Barbato was born in Santiago-Chile in 1983. As a poet he wrote The Pillars of Creation and he often publish magazines from Italy, Switzerland, Mexico, Chile, Ecuador and more. He participates in the Slam Poetry with poets from Italy and Switzerland. Barbato is the founder of Poetic Unrealism, is a movement of creators from different countries traying to make a difference and make a way to arrive to transcendence. Recently he was translated for a special magazine called Greece anthology of young poets from Italian part of Switzerland. Also, he was been translated to the hindi for the Kritya Poetry Journal.

Through The Wall

A man and his shadow
A shadow without eyes
Eyes to pocket
Lonely road
Heading to the soul
A mountain
Abandoned
Waiting for me
The man
Looks at me
I break
The mirrors
He is still in his corner
The shadow is me
A stain
About the
Walls
Of the
Mind
On fire
Someone's
That dreams to me
Or invent me about
A blank sheet
My nature
It is of letters
Bones
And veins
They are rivers
Words
That come down
That open
Like roads
About the life that barks at me
About the death that awaits me.

Turn Your Eyes

My dreams

Go away by my eyes

When I'm sleeping

They back home

And show me

How I've to

Write

About my

Burning

Soul

My Secret, The Sun

I have a secret
A small one
Is inside
My eyes
But if
You
Wanna take a look here
You must to know
How to fight
Against my
Burning
Mind
Because
Some people
Already trayed
But all of them
Found just the fire
So
My secret
The smallest one
that I have, is crying
It ask me for the light
But I have just ashes
Ashes and a dirty
Darkness behind
My tired back
My secret
Is my soul
And I'm gonna
Share it with you
Just after I died

Izabela
Zubko

Izabela Zubko – born in 1974 in Warsaw, Poland - poetess, journalist and translator. She is an author of 10 volumes of poetry. Her poems were published in many newspapers in Poland and abroad. They can be found in many anthologies, too. For example her works there are in the collection entitled "The poets of our time" and "Anthology of Slavic Poetry". She is a member of: the Union of Polish Writers (ZLP), the Polish Writer's Association of 2nd Warsaw Branch (SAP) and the Association of Culture Originators (RSTK).

You came

now I can get warm

my cold hands and feet

in the garden of your touch

swim freely

in the bay of words

sweet like black cherries

dance in the teardrop

treading upon discontent's

heels

you came like the good fire

that melts the darkness

like the flame that consummates

translated by: Anna Mazur

The Viewing

I'm standing on the veil of light
and I'm looking from under its shadow
at the changing colors
of those several words about us

untangled from the comet's tail
a request to life
is wrapping around the loom of film
of the stopped future

it speaks with silence of
dancing with the wind force
flashes of our glances
staring at the sun

translated by: Anna Mazur

A Lighthouse keeper

you are the motion of my hands

the voice of shut mouth

and the mystery

warming up a frigid night

stealthily in drowse

we stumble

on bare shadows

I braided a footbridge from them

over an unflowing river

translated by: Anna Mazur

Remembering

our fallen soldiers of verse

Janet Perkins Caldwell
February 14, 1959 ~ September 20, 2016

Alan W. Jankowski
16 March 1961 ~ 10 March 2017

Now available

1 April 2020

World Healing World Peace
2020

Poets for Humanity

Inner Child Press
News

Poetry Posse Members

We are so excited to share and announce a few of the current books, as well as the new and upcoming books of some of our Poetry Posse authors.

On the following pages we present to you ...

Jackie Davis Allen

Gail Weston Shazor

hülya n. yılmaz

Nizar Sartawi

Faleeha Hassan

Fahredin Shehu

Caroline 'Ceri' Nazareno

Eliza Segiet

William S. Peters, Sr.

COMING SOON
www.innerchildpress.com

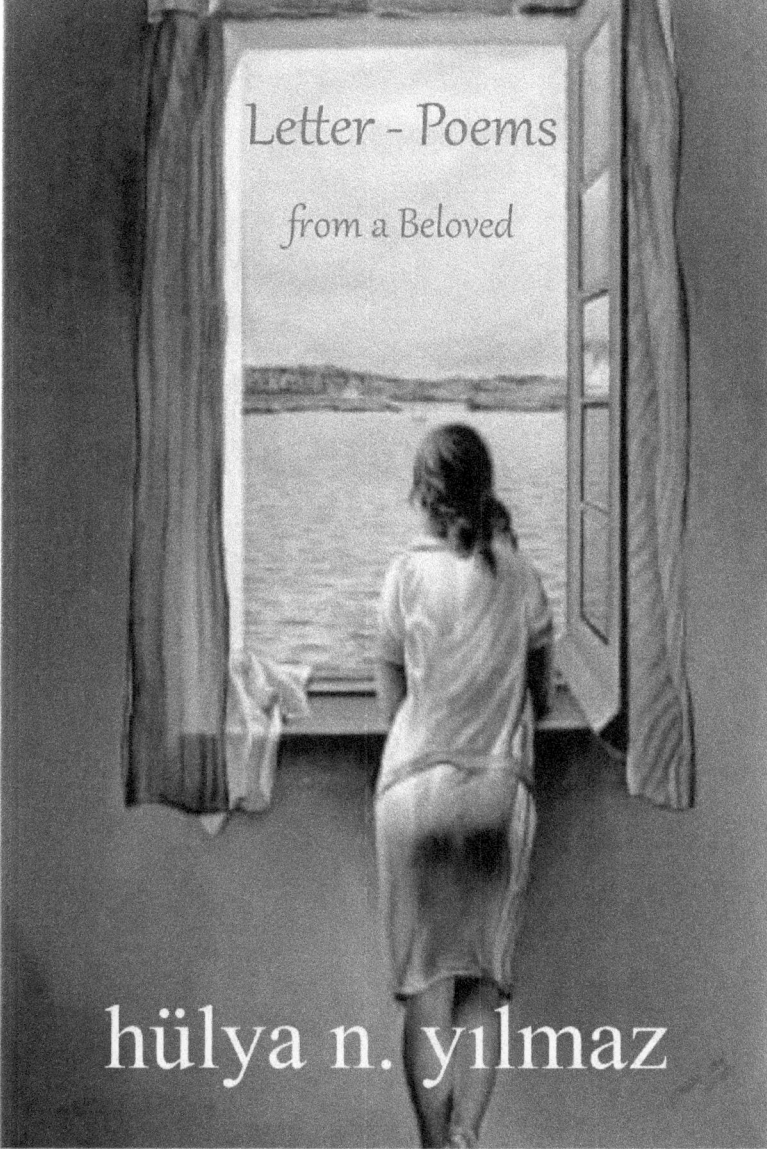

Letter - Poems

from a Beloved

hülya n. yılmaz

Inner Child Press News

COMING SOON

www.innerchildpress.com

The Book of krisar

volume v

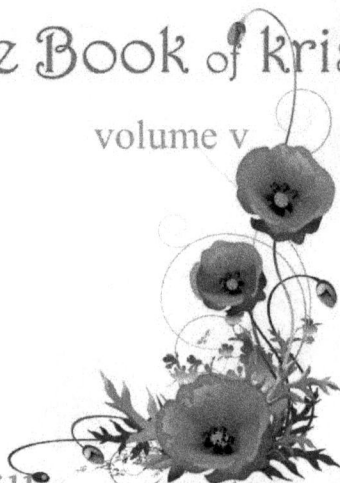

william s. peters, sr.

Now Available
www.innerchildpress.com

The Book of krisar

Volume I

william s. peters, sr.

The Book of krisar

Volume II

william s. peters, sr.

Now Available

www.innerchildpress.com

The Book of krisar

Volume III

william s. peters, sr.

The Book of krisar

Volume IV

william s. peters, sr.

Now Available

www.innerchildpress.com

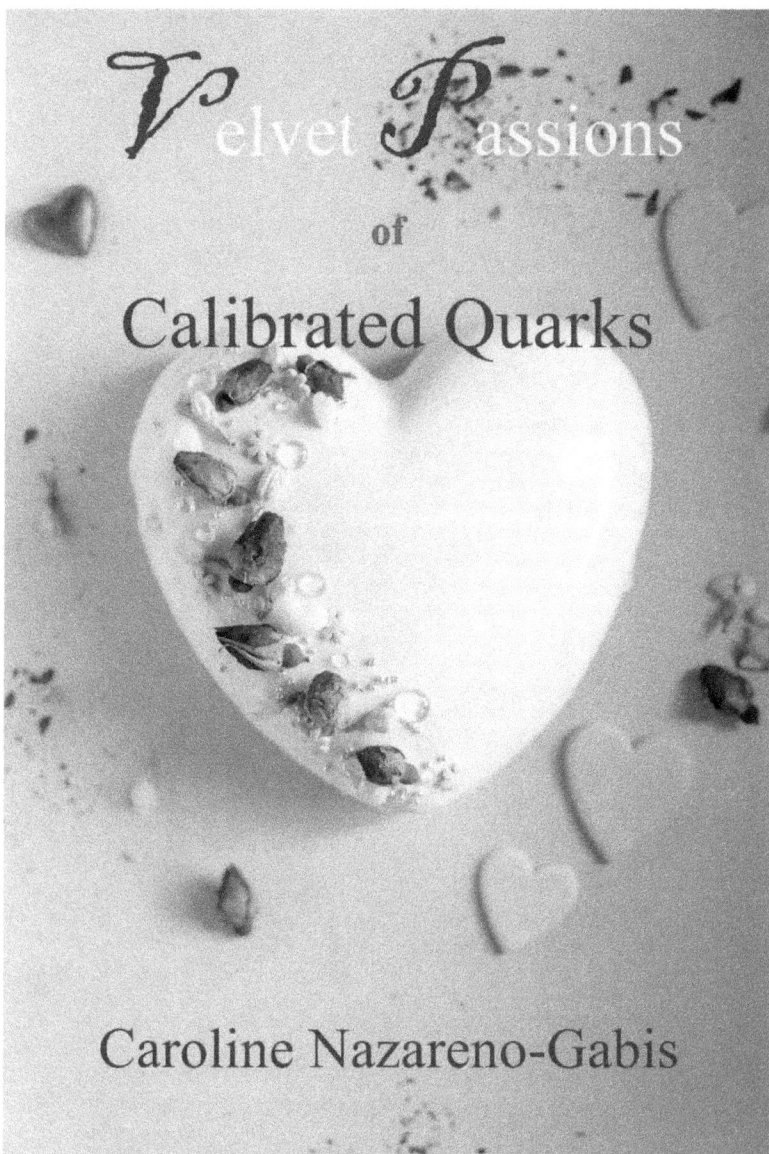

Velvet Passions

of

Calibrated Quarks

Caroline Nazareno-Gabis

Inner Child Press News

Now Available
www.innerchildpress.com

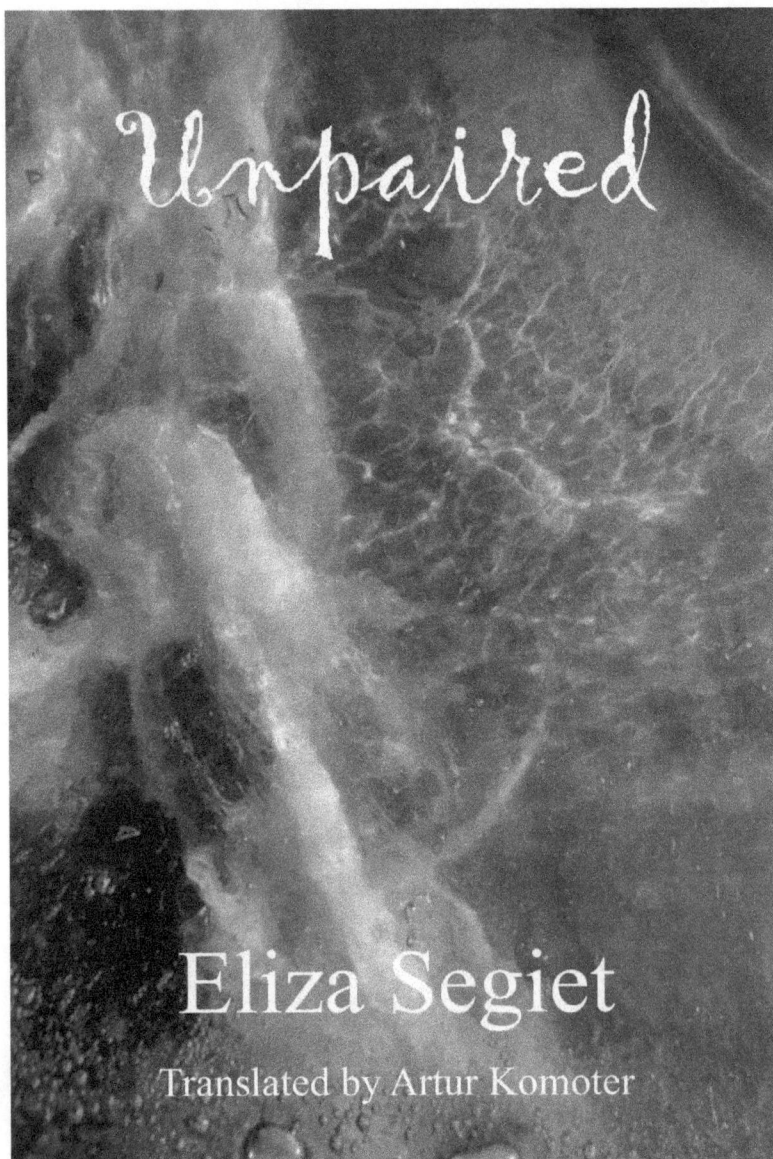

Unpaired

Eliza Segiet

Translated by Artur Komoter

Private Issue

www.innerchildpress.com

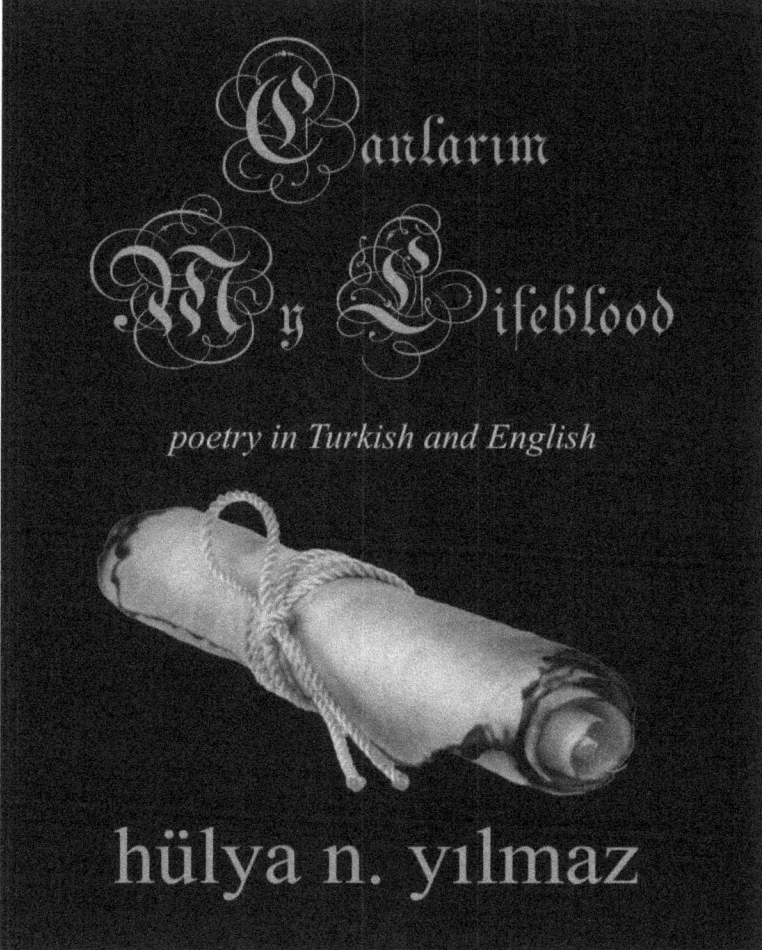

Canlarım
My Lifeblood

poetry in Turkish and English

hülya n. yılmaz

Now Available

www.innerchildpress.com

Butterfly's Voice

Faleeha Hassan

Translated by William M. Hutchins

Now Available at
www.innerchildpress.com

No Illusions

Through the Looking Glass

Jackie Davis Allen

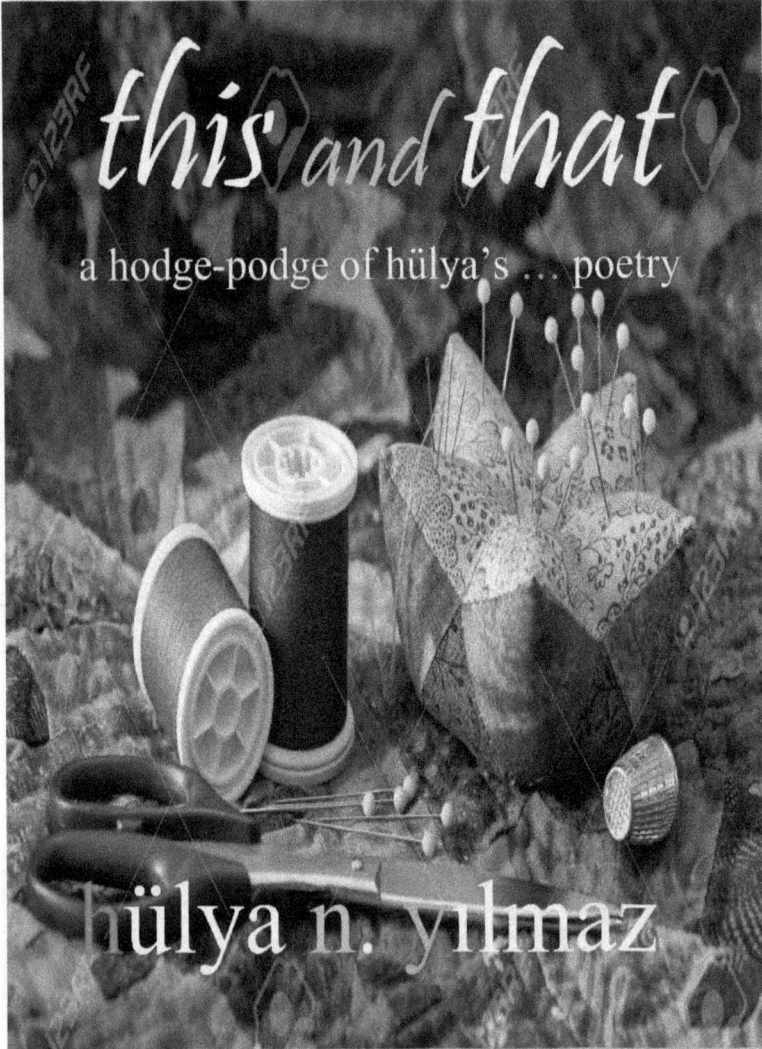

this and that

a hodge-podge of hülya's ... poetry

hülya n. yılmaz

Now Available at

www.innerchildpress.com

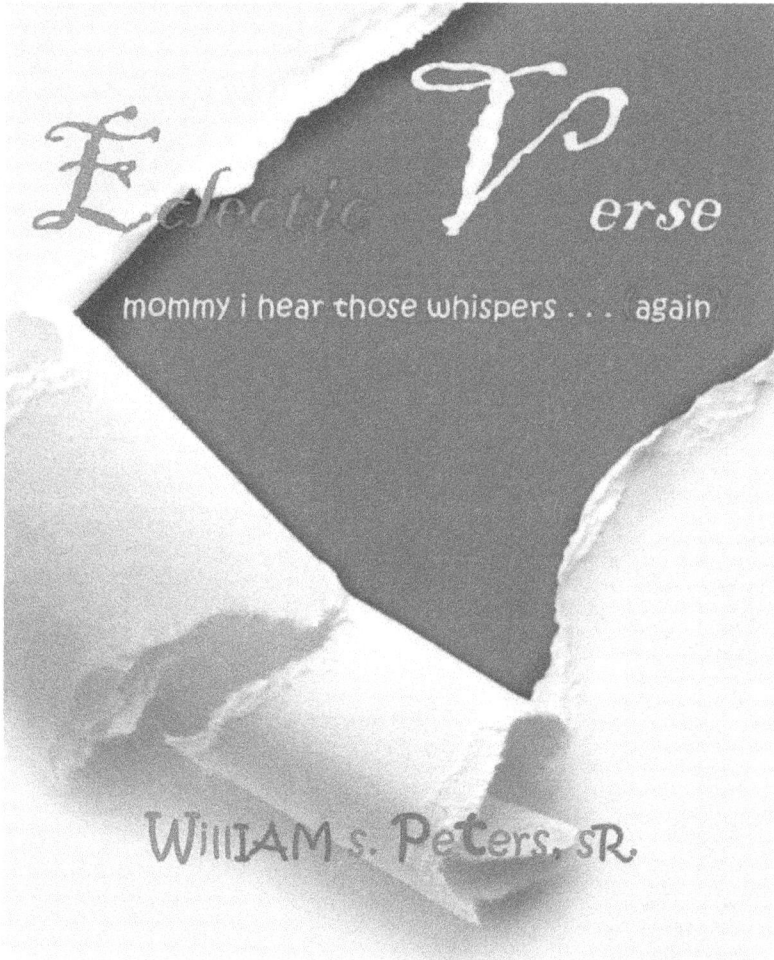

Eclectic Verse

mommy i hear those whispers . . . again

WilliAM s. PeTers, sR.

Inner Child Press News

Now Available at
www.innerchildpress.com

HERENOW

FAHREDIN SHEHU

Now Available at
www.innerchildpress.com

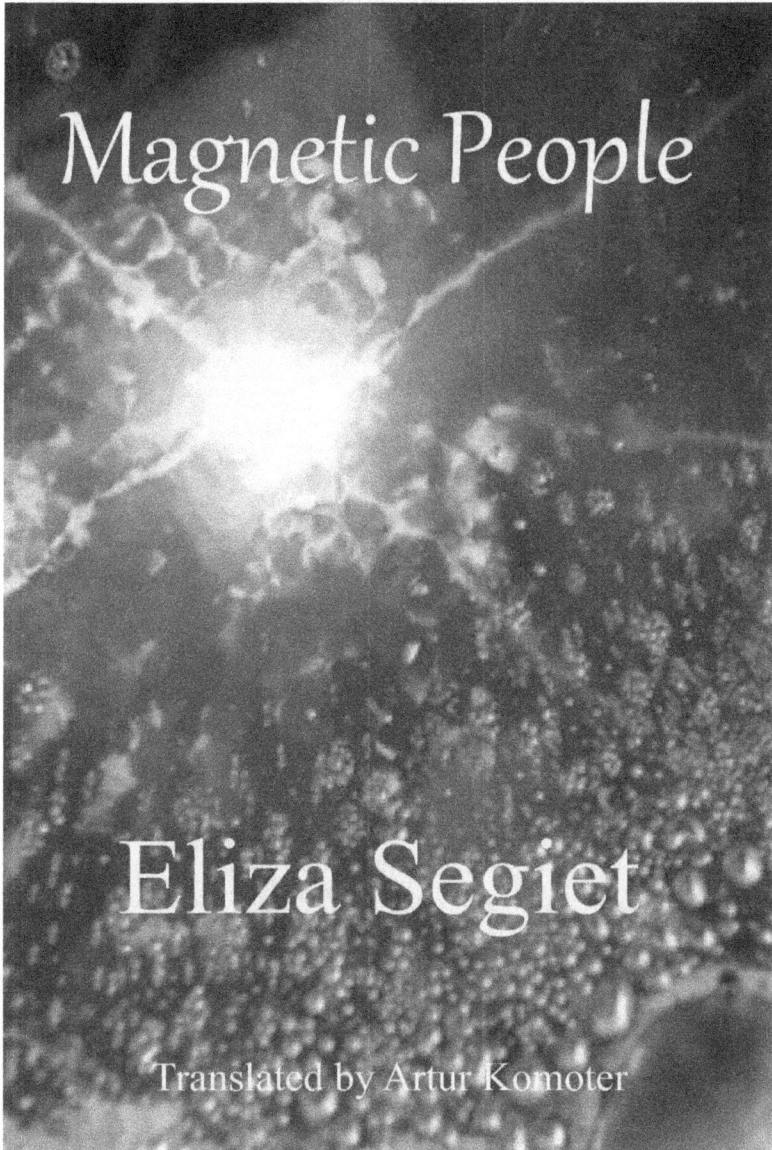

Magnetic People

Eliza Segiet

Translated by Artur Komoter

Dark Side
of the
Moon

Jackie Davis Allen

Now Available at
www.innerchildpress.com

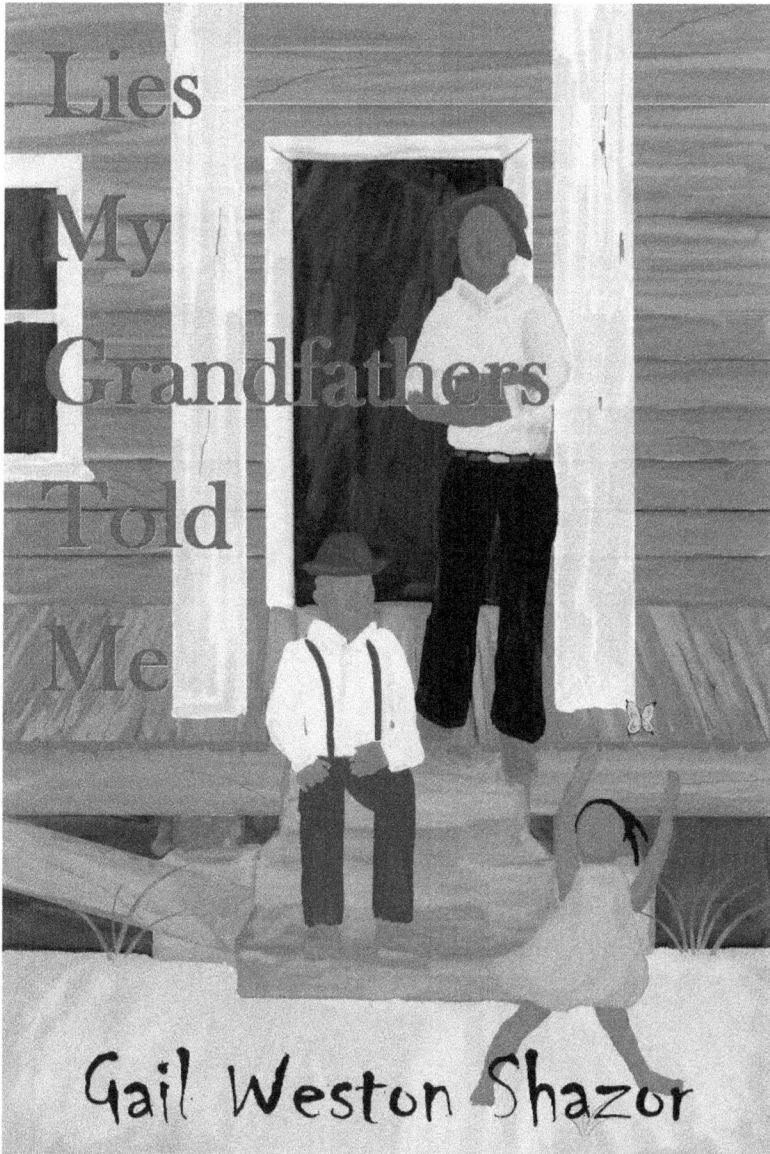

Lies
My
Grandfathers
Told
Me

Gail Weston Shazor

Now Available at
www.innerchildpress.com

Aflame

Memoirs in Verse

hülya n. yılmaz

Now Available at
www.innerchildpress.com

My Shadow

Nizar Sartawi

Inner Child Press News

Now Available at
www.innerchildpress.com

Now Available at
www.innerchildpress.com

Breakfast

for

Butterflies

Faleeha Hassan

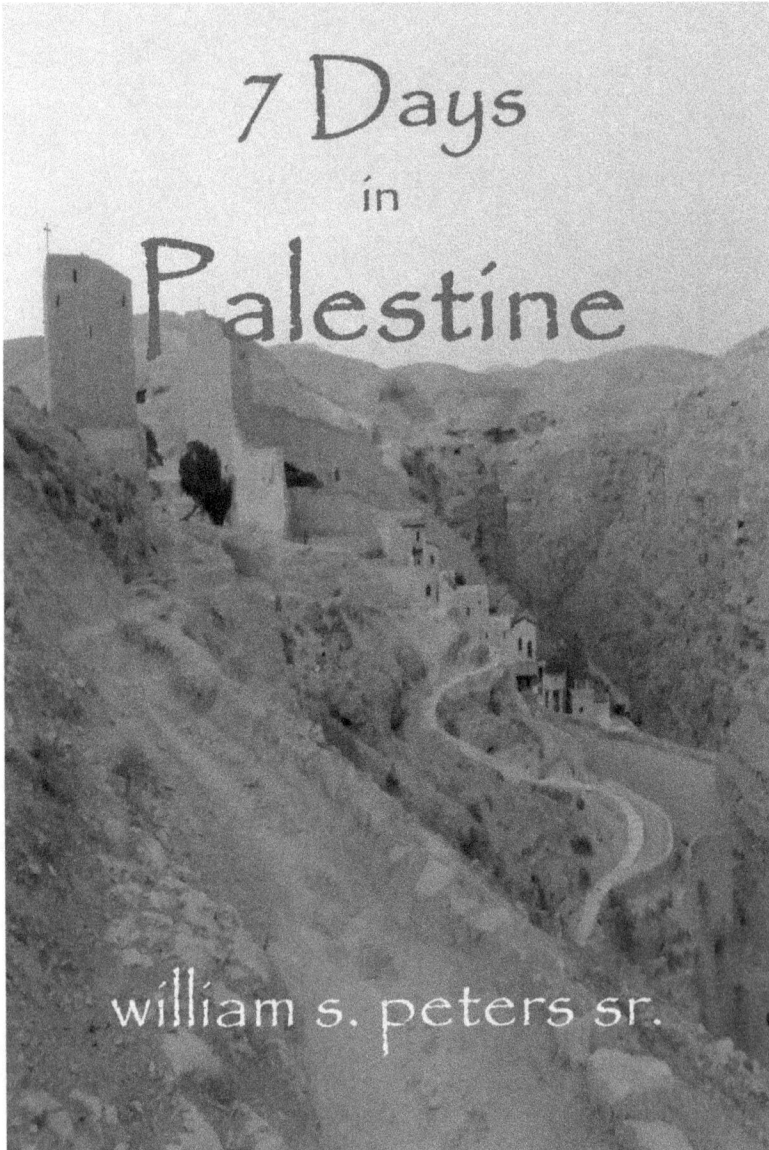

Now Available at
www.innerchildpress.com

inner child press
presents

Tunisia My Love

william s. peters, sr.

Coming in the Summer of 2020

The Journey

Footprints and Shadows

Kosovo

Tunisia

Macedonia

Morocco

Jordan

Palestine

Israel

Italy

Turkey

a collection of poetry inspired during my travels

william s. peters, sr.

Now Available at
www.innerchildpress.com

Inner Child Press News

Now Available at
www.innerchildpress.com

Inward Reflections

Think on These Things
Book II

william s. peters, sr.

Other

Anthological

works from

Inner Child Press International

www.innerchildpress.com

World Healing World Peace
2020

Poets for Humanity

Now Available

www.worldhealingworldpeacepoetry.com

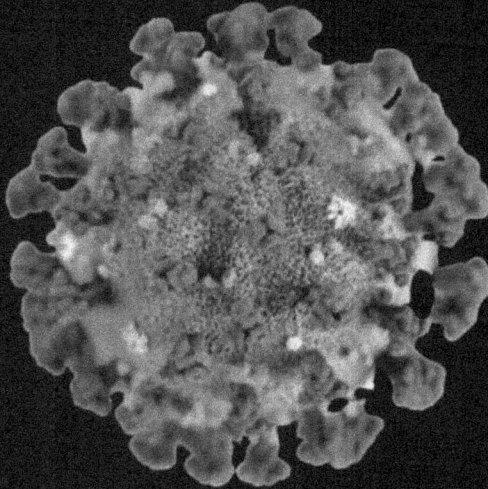

COMING SOON
www.innerchildpress.com

Poetry
from the
Balkans

The Balkan Poets

Now Available at
www.innerchildpress.com

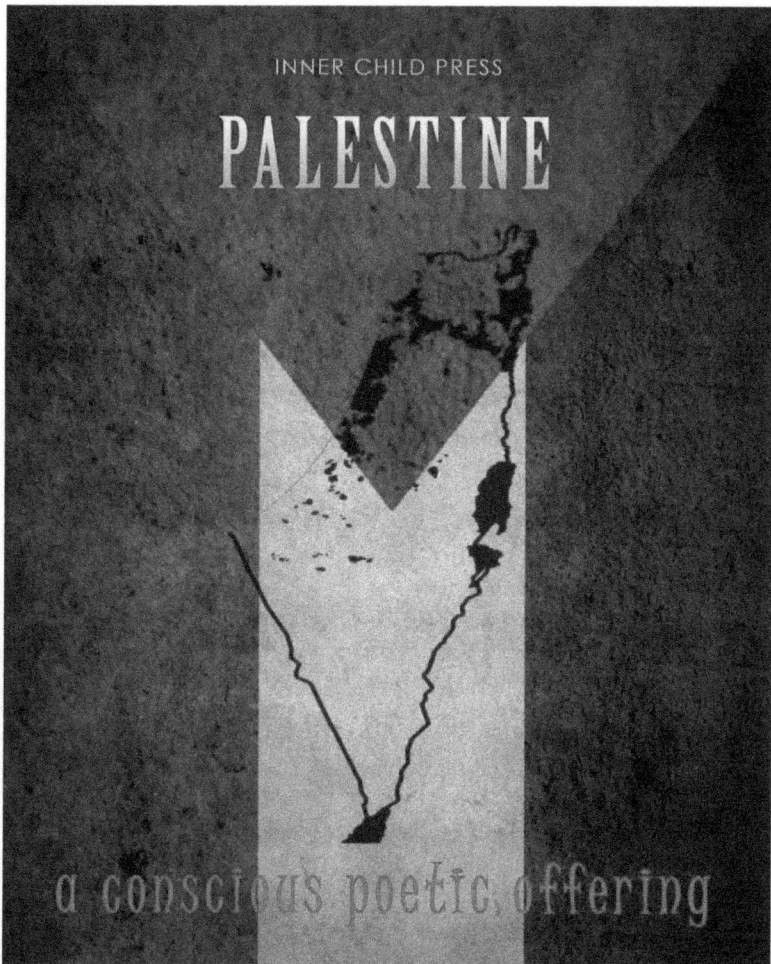

INNER CHILD PRESS

PALESTINE

a conscious poetic offering

Now Available at
www.innerchildpress.com

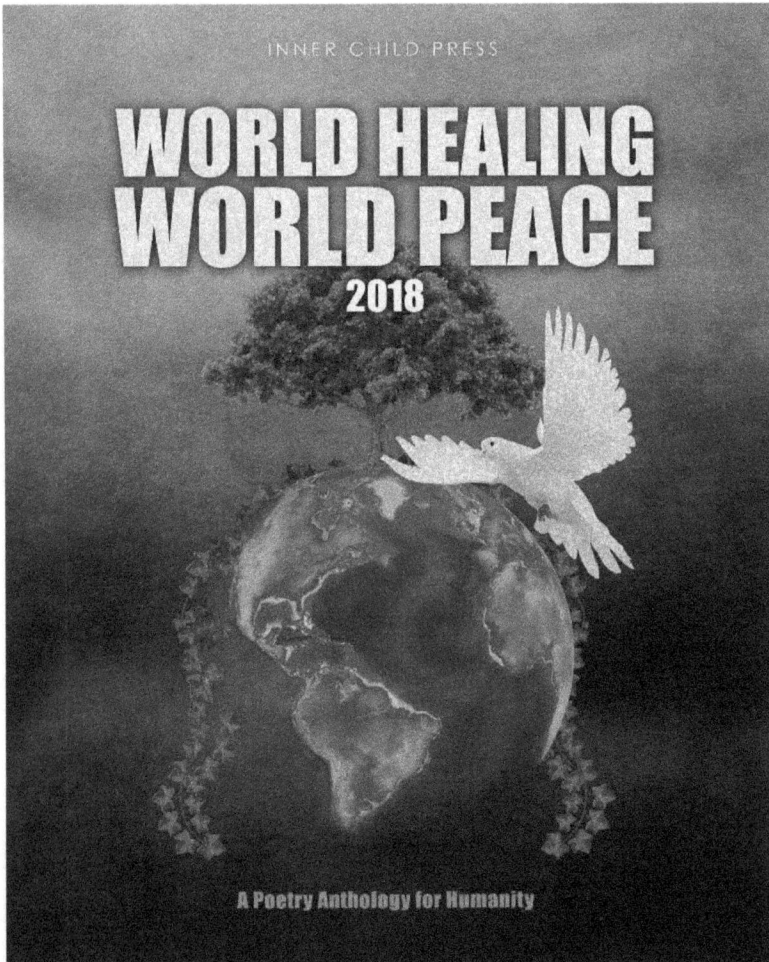

Inner Child Press International
presents

A Love Anthology
2019

The Love Poets

Now Available

www.worldhealingworldpeacepoetry.com

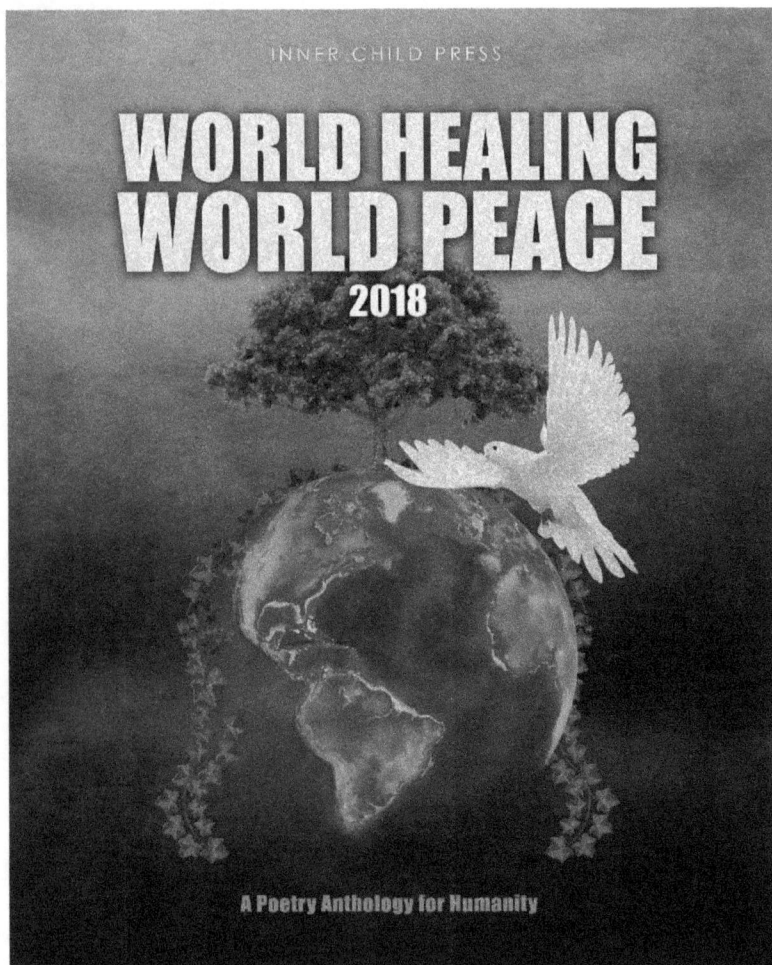

INNER CHILD PRESS

WORLD HEALING WORLD PEACE
2018

A Poetry Anthology for Humanity

Now Available

www.worldhealingworldpeacepoetry.com

Now Available

www.worldhealingworldpeacepoetry.com

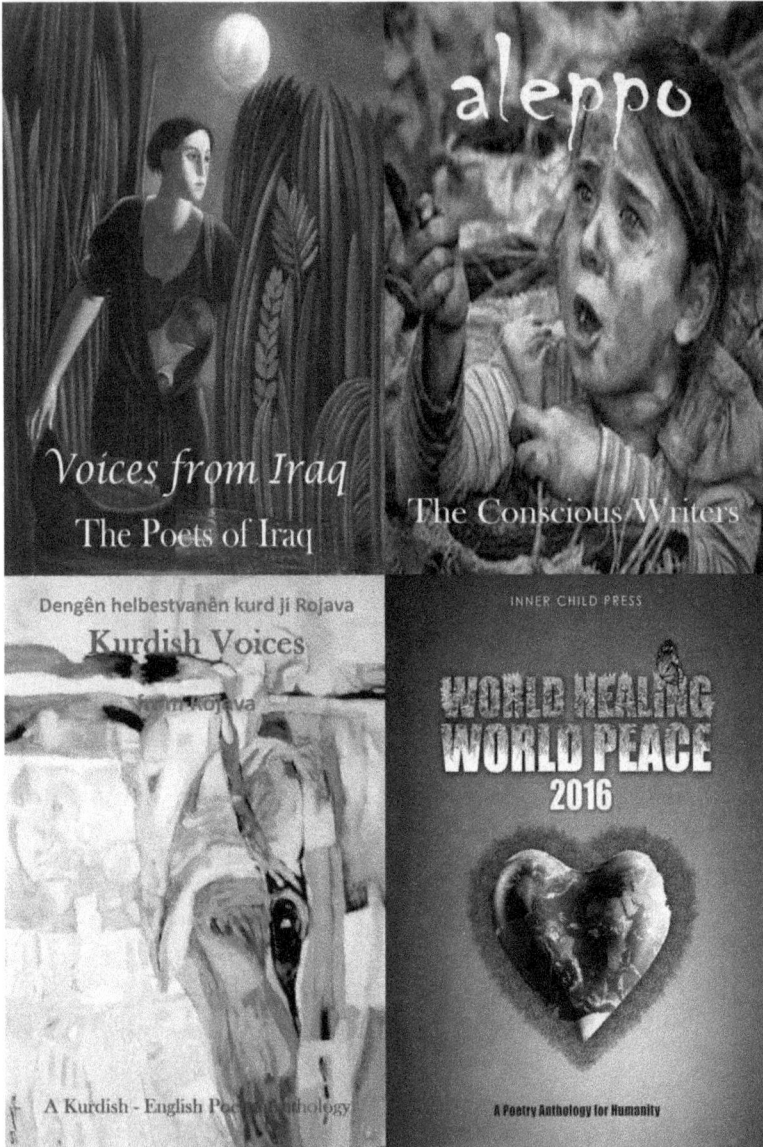

Now Available

www.innerchildpress.com/anthologies

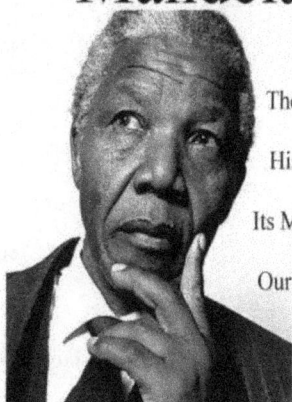

Now Available

www.innerchildpress.com/anthologies

i
want my
PoEtRy
to . . .

a collection of the Voices of Many inspired by . . .

Monte Smith

a collection of the Voices of Many inspired by . . .

Monte Smith

i
want my
PoEtRy
to . . .

volume II

i
want
my
PoEtRy
to . . . volume 3

a collection of the Voices of Many inspired by . . .

Monte Smith

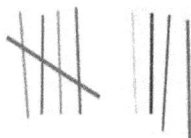

11 Words

(9 lines . . .)

for those who are challenged

an anthology of Poetry inspired by . . .

Poetry Dancer

Now Available

www.innerchildpress.com/anthologies

The Year of the Poet
January 2014

The Poetry Posse

Jamie Bond
Gail Weston Shazor
Albert 'Infinite' Carrasco
Siddartha Beth Pierce
Janet P. Caldwell
June 'Bugg' Barefield
Debbie M. Allen
Tony Henninger
Joe DaVerbal Minddancer
Robert Gibbons
Neetu Wali
Shareef Abdur-Rasheed
William S. Peters, Sr.

Carnation

Our January Feature
Terri L. Johnson

the Year of the Poet
February 2014

violets

The Poetry Posse
Jamie Bond
Gail Weston Shazor
Albert 'Infinite' Carrasco
Siddartha Beth Pierce
Janet P. Caldwell
June 'Bugg' Barefield
Debbie M. Allen
Tony Henninger
Joe DaVerbal Minddancer
Robert Gibbons
Neetu Wali
Shareef Abdur-Rasheed
William S. Peters, Sr.

Our February Features
Teresa E. Gallion & Robert Gibson

the Year of the Poet
March 2014

The Poetry Posse
Jamie Bond
Gail Weston Shazor
Albert 'Infinite' Carrasco
Siddartha Beth Pierce
Janet P. Caldwell
June 'Bugg' Barefield
Debbie M. Allen
Tony Henninger
Joe DaVerbal Minddancer
Robert Gibbons
Neetu Wali
Shareef Abdur-Rasheed
Kimberly Burnham
William S. Peters, Sr.

daffodil

Our March Featured Poets
Alicia C. Cooper & Hülya yılmaz

the Year of the Poet
April 2014

The Poetry Posse
Jamie Bond
Gail Weston Shazor
Albert 'Infinite' Carrasco
Siddartha Beth Pierce
Janet P. Caldwell
June 'Bugg' Barefield
Debbie M. Allen
Tony Henninger
Joe DaVerbal Minddancer
Robert Gibbons
Neetu Wali
Shareef Abdur-Rasheed
Kimberly Burnham
William S. Peters, Sr.

Our April Featured Poets
Fahredin Shehu
Martina Reisz Newberry
Justin Blackburn
Monte Smith

Sweet Pea

celebrating international poetry month

Now Available

www.innerchildpress.com/the-year-of-the-poet

the year of the poet
May 2014

May's Featured Poets
ReeCee
Joski the Poet
Shannon Stanton

Dedicated to our Children

The Poetry Posse
Jamie Bond
Gail Weston Shazor
Albert 'Infinite' Carrasco
Siddhartha 'Beth' Pierre
Janet P. Caldwell
Jesse 'Bugg' Barefield
Debbie M. Allen
Tony Henninger
Joe DaVerbal Minddancer
Robert Gibbons
Neetu Wali
Shareef Abdur-Rasheed
Kimberly Burnham
William S. Peters, Sr.

Lily of the Valley

the Year of the Poet
June 2014

Love & Relationship

Rose

June's Featured Poets
Shantelle McLin
Jacqueline D. E. Kennedy
Abraham N. Benjamin

The Poetry Posse
Jamie Bond
Gail Weston Shazor
Albert 'Infinite' Carrasco
Siddhartha Beth Pierce
Janet P. Caldwell
Jesse 'Bugg' Barefield
Debbie M. Allen
Tony Henninger
Joe DaVerbal Minddancer
Robert Gibbons
Neetu Wali
Shareef Abdur-Rasheed
Kimberly Burnham
William S. Peters, Sr.

The Year of the Poet
July 2014

July Feature Poets
Christena A. V. Williams
Dr. John R. Strum
Kolade Olanrewaju Freedom

The Poetry Posse
Jamie Bond
Gail Weston Shazor
Albert 'Infinite' Carrasco
Siddhartha Beth Pierce
Janet P. Caldwell
Jesse 'Bugg' Barefield
Debbie M. Allen
Tony Henninger
Joe DaVerbal Minddancer
Robert Gibbons
Neetu Wali
Shareef Abdur-Rasheed
Kimberly Burnham
William S. Peters, Sr.

Lotus
Asian Flower of the Month

The Year of the Poet
August 2014

Gladiolus

The Poetry Posse
Jamie Bond
Gail Weston Shazor
Albert 'Infinite' Carrasco
Siddhartha Beth Pierce
Janet P. Caldwell
Jesse 'Bugg' Barefield
Debbie M. Allen
Tony Henninger
Joe DaVerbal Minddancer
Robert Gibbons
Neetu Wali
Shareef Abdur-Rasheed
Kimberly Burnham
William S. Peters, Sr.

August Feature Poets
Ann White ✦ Rosalind Cherry ✦ Shelia Jenkins

Now Available

www.innerchildpress.com/the-year-of-the-poet

The Year of the Poet
September 2014

Aster   Morning-Glory

Wild Chicory - September's Birth Day Flower

September Feature Poets
Florence Malone * Keith Alan Hamilton

The Poetry Posse
Jamie Bond * Gail Weston Shazor * Albert 'Infinite' Carrasco * Siddartha Beth Pierce
Janet P. Caldwell * Suna 'Bugg' Barefield * Debbie M. Allen * Tony Henninger
Joe DaVerbal Minddancer * Robert Gibbons * Neetu Wali * Shareef Abdur-Rasheed
Kimberly Burnham * William S. Peters, Sr.

THE YEAR OF THE POET
October 2014

Red Poppy

The Poetry Posse
Jamie Bond * Gail Weston Shazor * Albert 'Infinite' Carrasco * Siddartha Beth Pierce
Janet P. Caldwell * Suna 'Bugg' Barefield * Debbie M. Allen * Tony Henninger
Joe DaVerbal Minddancer * Robert Gibbons * Neetu Wali * Shareef Abdur-Rasheed
Kimberly Burnham * William S. Peters, Sr.

October Feature Poets
Ceri Naz * RaJendra Padhi * Elizabeth Castillo

THE YEAR OF THE POET
November 2014

Chrysanthemum

The Poetry Posse
Jamie Bond * Gail Weston Shazor * Albert 'Infinite' Carrasco * Siddartha Beth Pierce
Janet P. Caldwell * Suna 'Bugg' Barefield * Debbie M. Allen * Tony Henninger
Joe DaVerbal Minddancer * Robert Gibbons * Neetu Wali * Shareef Abdur-Rasheed
Kimberly Burnham * William S. Peters, Sr.

November Feature Poets
Jocelyn Mosman * Jackie Allen * James Moore * Neville Hiatt

The Year of the Poet
December 2014

Narcissus

The Poetry Posse
Jamie Bond
Gail Weston Shazor
Albert 'Infinite' Carrasco
Siddartha Beth Pierce
Janet P. Caldwell
Suna 'Bugg' Barefield
Debbie M. Allen
Tony Henninger
DaVerbal Minddancer
Robert Gibbons
Neetu Wali
Shareef Abdur-Rasheed
Kimberly Burnham
William S. Peters, Sr.

December Feature Poets
Katherine Wyatt* WrittenInflesh * Santosh Bakaya * Justin Hyde

Now Available

www.innerchildpress.com/the-year-of-the-poet

Now Available

www.innerchildpress.com/the-year-of-the-poet

The Year of the Poet II
May 2015

May's Featured Poets
Geri Algeri
Akin Mosi Chinneru
Anna Jakubezak

Emeralds

The Poetry Posse 2015

Janie Bond * Gail Weston Shazor * Albert 'Infinite' Carrasco
Siddartha Beth Pierce * Janet P. Caldwell * Tony Henninger
Joe DaVerbal Minddancer * Neetu Wali * Shareef Abdur - Rasheed
Kimberly Burnham * Ann White * Keith Alan Hamilton
Katherine Wyatt * Fahredin Shehu * Hülya N. Yılmaz
Teresa E. Gallion * Jackie Allen * William S. Peters, Sr.

The Year of the Poet II
June 2015

June's Featured Poets
Anahit Arustamyan * Yvette D. Murrell * Regina A. Walker

Pearl

The Poetry Posse 2015

Janie Bond * Gail Weston Shazor * Albert 'Infinite' Carrasco
Siddartha Beth Pierce * Janet P. Caldwell * Tony Henninger
Joe DaVerbal Minddancer * Neetu Wali * Shareef Abdur - Rasheed
Kimberly Burnham * Ann White * Keith Alan Hamilton
Katherine Wyatt * Fahredin Shehu * Hülya N. Yılmaz
Teresa E. Gallion * Jackie Allen * William S. Peters, Sr.

The Year of the Poet II
July 2015

The Featured Poets for July 2015
Abhik Shome * Christina Neal * Robert Neal

Rubies

The Poetry Posse 2015

Janie Bond * Gail Weston Shazor * Albert 'Infinite' Carrasco
Siddartha Beth Pierce * Janet P. Caldwell * Tony Henninger
Joe DaVerbal Minddancer * Neetu Wali * Shareef Abdur - Rasheed
Kimberly Burnham * Ann White * Keith Alan Hamilton
Katherine Wyatt * Fahredin Shehu * Hülya N. Yılmaz
Teresa E. Gallion * Jackie Allen * William S. Peters, Sr.

The Year of the Poet II
August 2015

Peridot

Featured Poets
Gayle Howell
Ann Chalasz
Christopher Schultz

The Poetry Posse 2015

Janie Bond * Gail Weston Shazor * Albert 'Infinite' Carrasco
Siddartha Beth Pierce * Janet P. Caldwell * Tony Henninger
Joe DaVerbal Minddancer * Neetu Wali * Shareef Abdur – Rasheed
Kimberly Burnham * Ann White * Keith Alan Hamilton
Katherine Wyatt * Fahredin Shehu * Hülya N. Yılmaz
Teresa E. Gallion * Jackie Allen * William S. Peters, Sr.

Now Available

www.innerchildpress.com/the-year-of-the-poet

The Year of the Poet II
September 2015

Featured Poets
Alfreda Ghee   Lonneice Weeks Badley   Demetrios Trifiatis

Sapphires

The Poetry Posse 2015
Jamie Bond * Gail Weston Shazor * Albert 'Infinite' Carrasco
Siddartha Beth Pierce * Janet P. Caldwell * Tony Henninger
Joe DaVerbal Minddancer * Neetu Wali * Shareef Abdur – Rasheed
Kimberly Burnham * Ann White * Keith Alan Hamilton
Katherine Wyatt * Fahredin Shehu * Hülya N. Yılmaz
Teresa E. Gallion * Jackie Allen * William S. Peters, Sr

The Year of the Poet II
October 2015

Featured Poets
Monte Smith * Laura J Wolfe * William Washington

Opal

The Poetry Posse 2015
Jamie Bond * Gail Weston Shazor * Albert 'Infinite' Carrasco
Siddartha Beth Pierce * Janet P. Caldwell * Tony Henninger
Joe DaVerbal Minddancer * Neetu Wali * Shareef Abdur – Rasheed
Kimberly Burnham * Ann White * Keith Alan Hamilton
Katherine Wyatt * Fahredin Shehu * Hülya N. Yılmaz
Teresa E. Gallion * Jackie Allen * William S. Peters, Sr.

The Year of the Poet II
November 2015

Featured Poets
Alan W. Jankowski
Branca Mohanty
James Moore

Topaz

The Poetry Posse 2015
Jamie Bond * Gail Weston Shazor * Albert 'Infinite' Carrasco
Siddartha Beth Pierce * Janet P. Caldwell * Tony Henninger
Joe DaVerbal Minddancer * Neetu Wali * Shareef Abdur – Rasheed
Kimberly Burnham * Ann White * Keith Alan Hamilton
Katherine Wyatt * Fahredin Shehu * Hülya N. Yılmaz
Teresa E. Gallion * Jackie Allen * William S. Peters, Sr.

The Year of the Poet II
December 2015

Featured Poets
Kerione Bryan * Michelle Joan Barulich * Neville Hiatt

Turquoise

The Poetry Posse 2015
Jamie Bond * Gail Weston Shazor * Albert 'Infinite' Carrasco
Siddartha Beth Pierce * Janet P. Caldwell * Tony Henninger
Joe DaVerbal Minddancer * Neetu Wali * Shareef Abdur – Rasheed
Kimberly Burnham * Ann White * Keith Alan Hamilton
Katherine Wyatt * Fahredin Shehu * Hülya N. Yılmaz
Teresa E. Gallion * Jackie Allen * William S. Peters, Sr.

Now Available

www.innerchildpress.com/the-year-of-the-poet

The Year of the Poet III
January 2016

Featured Poets
Lana Joseph * Atom Cyrus Rush * Christena Williams

Dark-eyed Junco

The Poetry Posse 2016

The Year of the Poet III
February 2016

Featured Poets
Anthony Arnold
Anna Chalasz
Andre Hawthorne

Puffin

The Poetry Posse 2016

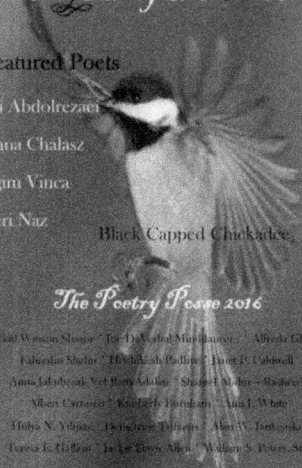

The Year of the Poet
March 2016
Featured Poets
Jeton Kelmendi   Nizar Sartawi   Sami Muhanna

Robin

The Poetry Posse 2016

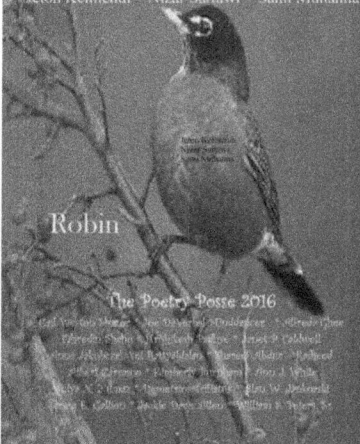

The Year of the Poet III

Featured Poets

Ali Abdolrezaei

Anna Chalasz

Agim Vinca

Ceri Naz

Black Capped Chickadee

The Poetry Posse 2016

celebrating international poetry month

Now Available

www.innerchildpress.com/the-year-of-the-poet

The Year of the Poet
May 2016

Bob Strum
Barbara Allan
D.L. Davis

Oriole

The Year of the Poet III
June 2016

Featured Poets

Qibrije Demiri- Frangu
Naime Beqiraj
Faleeha Hassan
Bedri Zyberaj

Black Necked Stilt

The Poetry Posse 2016

The Year of the Poet III
July

Iram Fatima 'Ashi'
Langley Shazor
Jody Doty
Emilia T. Davis

Indigo Bunting

The Poetry Posse 2016

The Year of the Poet III
August 2016

Featured Poets

Anita Dash
Irena Jovanovic
Malgorzata Gouluda

Painted Bunting

The Poetry Posse 2016

Now Available

www.innerchildpress.com/the-year-of-the-poet

The Year of the Poet III
September 2016

Featured Poets

Simone Weber
Abhijit Sen
Eunice Barbara C. Novio

Long Billed Corle

The Poetry Posse 2016

The Year of the Poet III
October 2016

Featured Poets

Fina Joseph
Krishnamurthy
James Moore

Barn Owl

The Poetry Posse 2016

The Year of the Poet III
November 2016

Featured Poets

Rosemary Burns
Robin Ouzman Hislop
Lonneice Weeks-Badley

Northern Cardinal

The Poetry Posse 2016

The Year of the Poet III
December 2016

Featured Poets

Samih Masoud
Mountassir Aziz Bien
Abdulkadir Musa

Rough Legged Hawk

The Poetry Posse 2016

Now Available

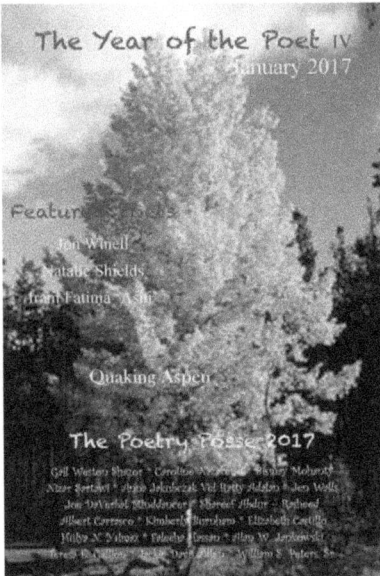

The Year of the Poet IV
January 2017

Featured Poets
Jen Winell
Natalie Shields
Irani Fatima Ashi

Quaking Aspen

The Poetry Posse 2017

The Year of the Poet IV
February 2017

Featured Poets
Lin Ross
Soukaina Fathi
Grwer Ghani

Witch Hazel

The Poetry Posse 2017

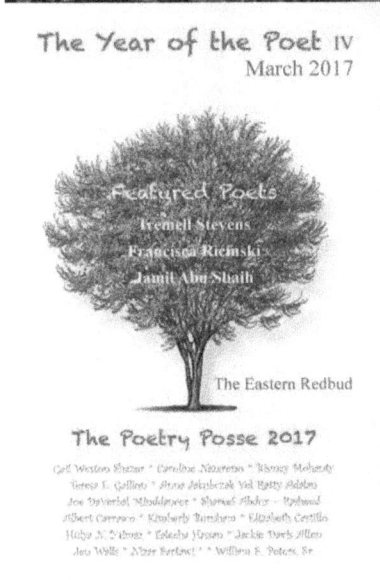

The Year of the Poet IV
March 2017

Featured Poets
Tremell Stevens
Francisca Riemski
Jamil Abu Shaih

The Eastern Redbud

The Poetry Posse 2017

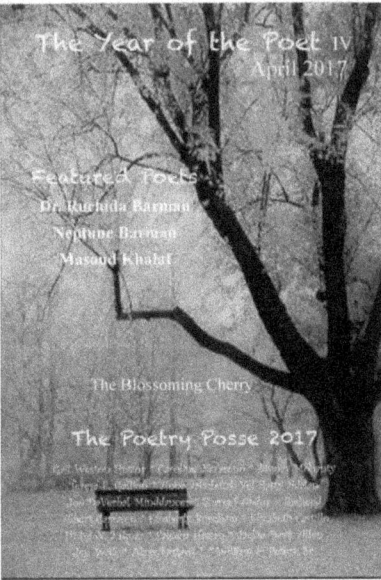

The Year of the Poet IV
April 2017

Featured Poets
Dr. Ruchida Barman
Neptune Barman
Masoud Khalaf

The Blossoming Cherry

The Poetry Posse 2017

Now Available

www.innerchildpress.com/the-year-of-the-poet

The Year of the Poet IV
May 2017

The Flowering Dogwood Tree

Featured Poets
Kallisa Powell
Alicja Maria Kuberska
Fethi Sassi

The Poetry Posse 2017

Gail Weston Shazor * Caroline Nazareno * Tzemin Mohanty
Teresa E. Gallion * Anna Jakubczak Vel Ratty Adalan
Jen DeVerbal Minddmoon * Shareef Abdur - Rasheed
Albert Carrasco * Kimberly Burnham * Elizabeth Castillo
Hülya N. Yılmaz * Eliesha Nelson * Jackie Davis Allen
Jen Walls * Nizar Sartawi * * William S. Peters, Sr.

The Year of the Poet IV
June 2017

Featured Poets
Elisa Seglet
Tze-Min Tsai
Abdulla Issa

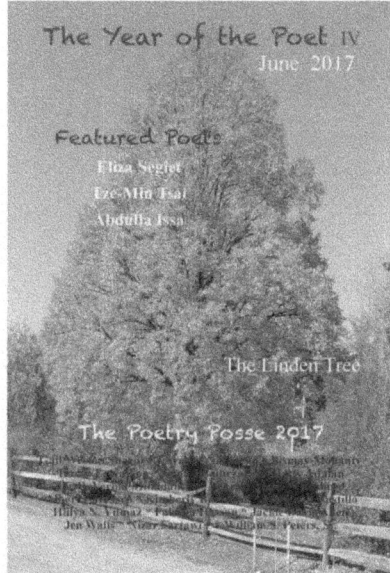

The Linden Tree

The Poetry Posse 2017

Hülya N. Yılmaz * Eliesha Nelson * Jackie Davis Allen
Jen Walls * Nizar Sartawi * * William S. Peters, Sr.

The Year of the Poet IV
July 2017

Featured Poets
Anca Mihaela Bruma
Ibaa Ismail
Zvonko Taneski

The Oak Moon

The Poetry Posse 2017

The Year of the Poet IV
August 2017

Featured Poets
Jonathan Aquino
Kitty Hsu
Langley Shazor

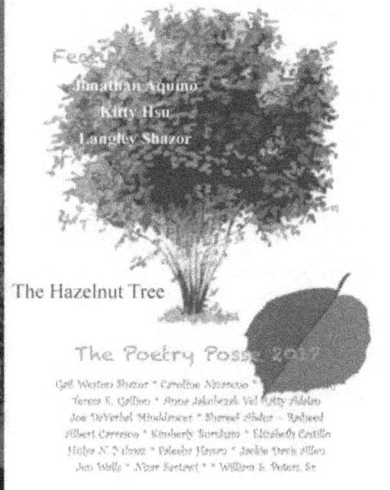

The Hazelnut Tree

The Poetry Posse 2017

Gail Weston Shazor * Caroline Nazareno *
Teresa E. Gallion * Anna Jakubczak Vel Ratty Adalan
Joe DeVerbal Minddmoon * Shareef Abdur - Rasheed
Albert Carrasco * Kimberly Burnham * Elizabeth Castillo
Hülya N. Yılmaz * Eliesha Nelson * Jackie Davis Allen
Jen Walls * Nizar Sartawi * * William S. Peters, Sr.

Now Available

www.innerchildpress.com/the-year-of-the-poet

The Year of the Poet IV
September 2017

Featured Poets

Martina Reisz Newberry
Ameer Nassir
Christine Fulco Neal
Robert Neal

The Elm Tree

The Poetry Posse 2017

Gail Weston Shazor * Caroline Nazareno * Bismay Mohanty
Teresa E. Gallion * Anna Jakubczak Vel Ratty Adalan
Joe DaVerbal Minddancer * Shareef Abdur – Rasheed
Albert Carrasco * Kimberly Burnham * Elizabeth Castillo
Hülya N. Yılmaz * Faleeha Hassan * Jackie Davis Allen
Jen Walls * Nizar Sartawi * * William S. Peters, Sr.

The Year of the Poet IV
October 2017

Featured Poets

Ahmed Abu Saleem
Nedal Al-Qaeim
Sadeddin Shahin

The Black Walnut Tree

The Poetry Posse 2017

Gail Weston Shazor * Caroline Nazareno * Bismay Mohanty
Teresa E. Gallion * Anna Jakubczak Vel Ratty Adalan
Joe DaVerbal Minddancer * Shareef Abdur – Rasheed
Albert Carrasco * Kimberly Burnham * Elizabeth Castillo
Hülya N. Yılmaz * Faleeha Hassan * Jackie Davis Allen
Jen Walls * Nizar Sartawi * * William S. Peters, Sr.

The Year of the Poet IV
November 2017

Featured Poets

Kay Peters
Alfreda D. Ghee
Gabriella Garofalo
Rosemary Cappello

The Tree of Life

The Poetry Posse 2017

Gail Weston Shazor * Caroline Nazareno * Bismay Mohanty
Teresa E. Gallion * Anna Jakubczak Vel Ratty Adalan
Joe DaVerbal Minddancer * Shareef Abdur – Rasheed
Albert Carrasco * Kimberly Burnham * Elizabeth Castillo
Hülya N. Yılmaz * Faleeha Hassan * Jackie Davis Allen
Jen Walls * Nizar Sartawi * William S. Peters, Sr.

The Year of the Poet IV
December 2017

Featured Poets

Justice Clarke
Mariel M. Pabroa
Kiley Brown

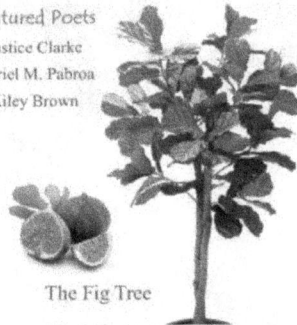

The Fig Tree

The Poetry Posse 2017

Gail Weston Shazor * Caroline Nazareno * Bismay Mohanty
Teresa E. Gallion * Anna Jakubczak Vel Ratty Adalan
Joe DaVerbal Minddancer * Shareef Abdur – Rasheed
Albert Carrasco * Kimberly Burnham * Elizabeth Castillo
Hülya N. Yılmaz * Faleeha Hassan * Jackie Davis Allen
Jen Walls * Nizar Sartawi * William S. Peters, Sr.

Now Available

www.innerchildpress.com/the-year-of-the-poet

The Year of the Poet V
January 2018
Featured Poets

Iyad Shamasnah
Yasmeen Hamzeh
Ali Abdolrezaei

Aksum

The Poetry Posse 2018
Gail Weston Shazor * Caroline Nazareno * Tezmin Ition Tsai
Hülya N. Yılmaz * Faleeha Hassan * Jackie Davis Allen
Teresa E. Gallion * Anna Jakubczak Vel Ratty Adalan
Alicja Maria Kubenska * Shareef Abdur – Rasheed
Kimberly Burnham * Elizabeth Castillo
Nizar Sartawi * William S. Peters, Sr.

The Year of the Poet V
February 2018

Sabean

Featured Poets
Muhammad Azram
Anna Szawracka
Abhilipsa Kumar
Aamika Aery

The Poetry Posse 2018
Gail Weston Shazor * Caroline Nazareno * Tezmin Ition Tsai
Hülya N. Yılmaz * Faleeha Hassan * Jackie Davis Allen
Teresa E. Gallion * Anna Jakubczak Vel Ratty Adalan
Alicja Maria Kubenska * Shareef Abdur – Rasheed
Kimberly Burnham * Elizabeth Castillo
Nizar Sartawi * William S. Peters, Sr.

The Year of the Poet V
March 2018

Featured Poets

Iram Fatima 'Ashi'
Cassandra Swan
Juleel Khuzaal
Sheria Zaman

Caribbean
&
Middle America

The Poetry Posse 2018
Gail Weston Shazor * Nizar Sartawi * Hülya N. Yılmaz
Jackie Davis Allen * Caroline 'Ceri' Nazareno
Alicja Maria Kubenska * Teresa E. Gallion
Faleeha Hassan * Shareef Abdur – Rasheed
Kimberly Burnham * Elizabeth Castillo
Tezmin Ition Tsai * William S. Peters, Sr.

The Year of the Poet V
April 2018
Featured Poets

The Nez Perce

The Poetry Posse 2018

Now Available

www.innerchildpress.com/the-year-of-the-poet

193

The Year of the Poet V
May 2018

Featured Poets

Zaldy Carreon de Leon Jr.
Sylvia K. Malpomuska
Emilia Adamisi
Ofelia Peshati

The Sumerians

The Poetry Posse 2018

Gail Weston Shazor * Nizar Sartawi * Hülya N. Yılmaz
Jackie Davis Allen * Caroline 'Ceri' Nazareno
Alicja Maria Kuberska * Teresa E. Gallion
Kimberly Burnham * Shareef Abdur – Rasheed
Faleeha Hassan * Elizabeth Castillo * Swapna Behera
Tezmin Ition Tsai * William S. Peters, Sr.

The Year of the Poet V
June 2018

Featured Poets

Bilall Maliqi * Daim Miftari * Gojko Božović * Sofija Živković

The Paleo Indians

The Poetry Posse 2018

Gail Weston Shazor * Nizar Sartawi * Hülya N. Yılmaz
Jackie Davis Allen * Caroline 'Ceri' Nazareno
Alicja Maria Kuberska * Teresa E. Gallion
Kimberly Burnham * Shareef Abdur – Rasheed
Faleeha Hassan * Elizabeth Castillo * Swapna Behera
Tezmin Ition Tsai * William S. Peters, Sr.

The Year of the Poet V
July 2018

Featured Poets

Panjali Irenee-Paddy
Mohammad Iqbal Harb
Eliza Seglet
Tom Higgins

Oceania

The Poetry Posse 2018

Gail Weston Shazor * Nizar Sartawi * Hülya N. Yılmaz
Jackie Davis Allen * Caroline 'Ceri' Nazareno
Alicja Maria Kuberska * Teresa E. Gallion
Kimberly Burnham * Shareef Abdur – Rasheed
Faleeha Hassan * Elizabeth Castillo * Swapna Behera
Tezmin Ition Tsai * William S. Peters, Sr.

The Year of the Poet V
August 2018

Featured Poets

Hussein Habasch * Mircea Dan Duta * Naida Mujkić * Swagat Das

The Lapita

The Poetry Posse 2018

Gail Weston Shazor * Nizar Sartawi * Hülya N. Yılmaz
Jackie Davis Allen * Caroline 'Ceri' Nazareno
Alicja Maria Kuberska * Teresa E. Gallion
Kimberly Burnham * Shareef Abdur – Rasheed
Ashok K. Bhargava * Elizabeth Castillo * Swapna Behaera
Tezmin Ition Tsai * William S. Peters, Sr.

Now Available

www.innerchildpress.com/the-year-of-the-poet

The Year of the Poet V
September 2018

The Aztecs & Incas

Featured Poets
Kolade Olanrewaju Freedom
Eliza Segiet
Muthet Bustami Abdul Ghani
Lily Swarn

The Poetry Posse 2018

Gail Weston Shazor * Nizar Sartawi * Hülya N. Yılmaz
Jackie Davis Allen * Caroline 'Ceri' Nazareno
Alicja Maria Kuberska * Teresa E. Gallion
Kimberly Burnham * Shareef Abdur – Rasheed
Ashok K. Bhargava * Elizabeth Castillo * Swapna Behera
Tezmin Ition Tsai * William S. Peters, Sr.

The Year of the Poet V
October 2018

Featured Poets
Alicia Minjarez * Lonneice Weeks-Badley
Lopamudra Mishra * Abdelwahed Souayah

Bengali

The Poetry Posse 2018

Gail Weston Shazor * Nizar Sartawi * Hülya N. Yılmaz
Jackie Davis Allen * Caroline 'Ceri' Nazareno
Alicja Maria Kuberska * Teresa E. Gallion
Kimberly Burnham * Shareef Abdur – Rasheed
Ashok K. Bhargava * Elizabeth Castillo * Swapna Behera
Tezmin Ition Tsai * William S. Peters, Sr.

The Year of the Poet V
November 2018

Featured Poets
Michelle Joan Barulich * Monsif Beroual
Krystyna Konecka * Nassira Nezzar

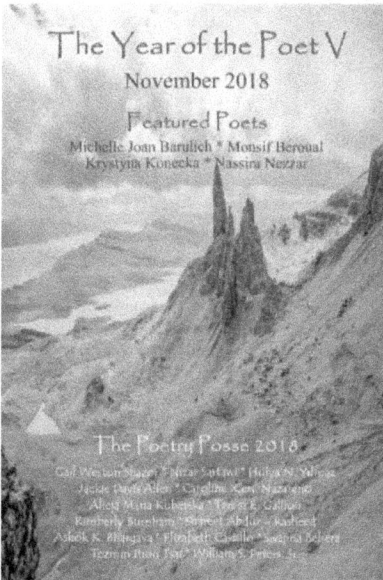

The Poetry Posse 2018

Gail Weston Shazor * Nizar Sartawi * Hülya N. Yılmaz
Jackie Davis Allen * Caroline 'Ceri' Nazareno
Alicja Maria Kuberska * Teresa E. Gallion
Kimberly Burnham * Shareef Abdur – Rasheed
Ashok K. Bhargava * Elizabeth Castillo * Swapna Behera
Tezmin Ition Tsai * William S. Peters, Sr.

The Year of the Poet V
December 2018

Featured Poets
Rose Terranova Cirigliano
Joanna Kalinowska
Sokulović Emir
Dr. T. Ashok Chakravarthy

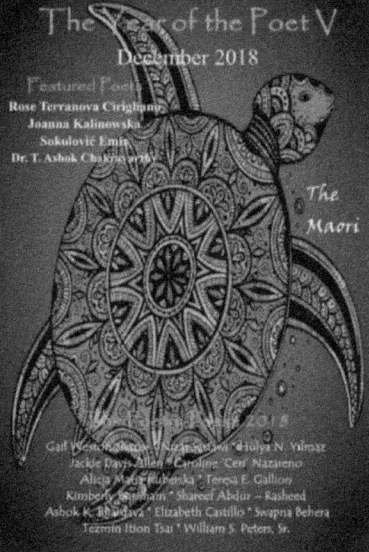

The Maori

The Poetry Posse 2018

Gail Weston Shazor * Nizar Sartawi * Hülya N. Yılmaz
Jackie Davis Allen * Caroline 'Ceri' Nazareno
Alicja Maria Kuberska * Teresa E. Gallion
Kimberly Burnham * Shareef Abdur – Rasheed
Ashok K. Bhargava * Elizabeth Castillo * Swapna Behera
Tezmin Ition Tsai * William S. Peters, Sr.

Now Available

www.innerchildpress.com/the-year-of-the-poet

The Year of the Poet V I
January 2019

Indigenous North Americans

Featured Poets

Houda Elfchtali
Anthony Briscoe
Iram Fatima 'Ashi'
Dr. K. K. Mathew

Dream Catcher

The Poetry Posse 2019

Gail Weston Shazor * Joe Paire * Hülya N. Yilmaz
Jackie Davis Allen * Caroline 'Ceri' Nazareno
Alicja Maria Kubeoska * Teresa E. Gallion
Kimberly Burnham * Shareef Abdur – Rasheed
Ashok K. Bhargava * Elizabeth Castillo * Swapna Behera
Tezmin Ition Tsai * William S. Peters, Sr.

The Year of the Poet VI
February 2019

Featured Poets

Marek Lukaszewicz * Bharati Nayak
Aida G. Roque * Jean-Jacques Fournier

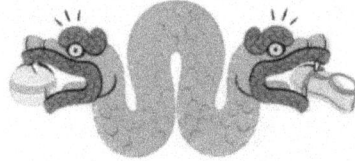

Meso-America

The Poetry Posse 2019

Gail Weston Shazor * Albert Carrasco * Hülya N. Yilmaz
Jackie Davis Allen * Caroline Nazareno * Eliza Segiet
Alicja Maria Kubenska * Teresa E. Gallion * Joe Paire
Kimberly Burnham * Shareef Abdur – Rasheed
Ashok K. Bhargava * Elizabeth Castillo * Swapna Behera
Tezmin Ition Tsai * William S. Peters, Sr.

The Year of the Poet VI
March 2019

Featured Poets

Enesa Mahmić * Sylwia K. Malinowska
Shurouk Hammoud * Anwer Ghani

The Caribbean

The Poetry Posse 2019

Gail Weston Shazor * Albert Carrasco * Hülya N. Yilmaz
Jackie Davis Allen * Caroline Nazareno * Eliza Segiet
Alicja Maria Kubenska * Teresa E. Gallion * Joe Paire
Kimberly Burnham * Shareef Abdur – Rasheed
Ashok K. Bhargava * Elizabeth Castillo * Swapna Behera
Tezmin Ition Tsai * William S. Peters, Sr.

The Year of the Poet VI
April 2019

Featured Poets

DL Davis * Michelle Joan Baruloch
Luiëzim Haziri * Faleeha Hassan

Central & West Africa

The Poetry Posse 2019

Gail Weston Shazor * Albert Carrasco * Hülya N. Yilmaz
Jackie Davis Allen * Caroline Nazareno * Eliza Segiet
Alicja Maria Kubenska * Teresa E. Gallion * Joe Paire
Kimberly Burnham * Shareef Abdur – Rasheed
Ashok K. Bhargava * Elizabeth Castillo * Swapna Behera
Tezmin Ition Tsai * William S. Peters, Sr.

Now Available

www.innerchildpress.com/the-year-of-the-poet

The Year of the Poet VI
May 2019
Featured Poets
Emad Al-Haydary * Hussein Nasser Jabr
Wahab Sheriff * Abdul Razzaq Al Ameeri

Asia Southeast Asia and Maritime Asia

The Poetry Posse 2019
Gail Weston Shazor * Albert Carrasco * Hülya N. Yılmaz
Jackie Davis Allen * Caroline Nazareno * Eliza Segiet
Alicja Maria Kuberska * Teresa E. Gallion * Joe Paire
Kimberly Burnham * Shareef Abdur – Rasheed
Ashok K. Bhargava * Elizabeth Castillo * Swapna Behera
Tezmin Ition Tsai * William S. Peters, Sr.

The Year of the Poet VI
June 2019
Featured Poets
Kate Gaudi Powiekszone * Sahaj Sabharwal
Iwu Jeff * Mohamed Abdel Aziz Shmeis

Arctic
Circumpolar

The Poetry Posse 2019
Gail Weston Shazor * Albert Carrasco * Hülya N. Yılmaz
Jackie Davis Allen * Caroline Nazareno * Eliza Segiet
Alicja Maria Kuberska * Teresa E. Gallion * Joe Paire
Kimberly Burnham * Shareef Abdur – Rasheed
Ashok K. Bhargava * Elizabeth Castillo * Swapna Behera
Tezmin Ition Tsai * William S. Peters, Sr.

The Year of the Poet VI
Featured Poets
Saadeddin Shahin * Andy Scott
Fahredin Shehu * Alok Kumar Ray

The Horn of Africa

Ethiopia   Djibouti

Somalia   Eritrea

The Poetry Posse 2019
Gail Weston Shazor * Albert Carrasco * Hülya N. Yılmaz
Jackie Davis Allen * Caroline Nazareno * Eliza Segiet
Alicja Maria Kuberska * Teresa E. Gallion * Joe Paire
Kimberly Burnham * Shareef Abdur – Rasheed
Ashok K. Bhargava * Elizabeth Castillo * Swapna Behera
Tezmin Ition Tsai * William S. Peters, Sr.

The Year of the Poet VI
August 2019
Featured Poets
Shola Balogun * Bharati Nayak
Monalisa Dash Dwibedy * Mbizo Chirasha

Coexist

Southwest Asia

The Poetry Posse 2019
Gail Weston Shazor * Albert Carrasco * Hülya N. Yılmaz
Jackie Davis Allen * Caroline Nazareno * Eliza Segiet
Alicja Maria Kuberska * Teresa E. Gallion * Joe Paire
Kimberly Burnham * Shareef Abdur – Rasheed
Ashok K. Bhargava * Elizabeth Castillo * Swapna Behera
Tezmin Ition Tsai * William S. Peters, Sr.

Now Available

www.innerchildpress.com/the-year-of-the-poet

197

The Year of the Poet VI
September 2019
Featured Poets
Elena Liliana Popescu * Gobinda Biswas
Iram Fatima 'Ashi' * Joseph S. Spence, Sr.
The Caucasus
The Poetry Posse 2019

The Year of the Poet VI
October 2019
Featured Poets
Ngozi Olivia Osuoha * Denisa Kondić
Pankhuri Sinha * Christena AV Williams
The Nile Valley
The Poetry Posse 2019

The Year of the Poet VI
November 2019
Featured Poets
Rozalie Aleksandrova * Orbindu Ganga
Smruti Ranjan Mohanty * Sofia Skleida
Northern Asia
The Poetry Posse 2019

The Year of the Poet VI
December 2019
Featured Poets
Rahul Kumar (Rachmani) * Sugra Paul
Bharati Nayak * Kapardeli Eftichia
Oceania
The Poetry Posse 2019

Now Available

www.innerchildpress.com/the-year-of-the-poet

The Year of the Poet VII
January 2020
Featured Poets
B S Tyagi * Ashok Chakravarthy Tholana
Andy Scott * Anwer Ghani

(90) Jean Henry Dunant and Frédéric Passy

The Year of Peace
Celebrating past Nobel Peace Prize Recipients

The Poetry Posse 2020
Gail Weston Shazor * Albert Carasco * Hülya N. Yilmaz
Jackie Davis Allen * Caroline Nazareno * Eliza Segiet
Alicja Maria Kubterska * Teresa E. Gallion * Joe Paire
Kimberly Burnham * Shareef Abdur – Rasheed
Ashok K. Bhargava * Elizabeth Castillo * Swapna Behera
Tezmin Ition Tsai * William S. Peters, Sr.

The Year of the Poet VII
February 2020
Featured Poets
Jennifer Ades * Martina Reisz Newberry
Ibrahim Honjo * Claudia Piccinno

Henri La Fontaine ~ 1913

The Year of Peace
Celebrating past Nobel Peace Prize Recipients

The Poetry Posse 2020
Gail Weston Shazor * Albert Carasco * Hülya N. Yilmaz
Jackie Davis Allen * Caroline Nazareno * Eliza Segiet
Alicja Maria Kubterska * Teresa E. Gallion * Joe Paire
Kimberly Burnham * Shareef Abdur – Rasheed
Ashok K. Bhargava * Elizabeth Castillo * Swapna Behera
Tezmin Ition Tsai * William S. Peters, Sr.

The Year of the Poet VII
March 2020
Featured Poets
Aziz Mountassir * Krishna Parana
Hannie Rouweler * Rozalia Aleksandrova

Aristide Briand ~ 1926 ~ Gustav Stresemann

The Year of Peace
Celebrating past Nobel Peace Prize Recipients

The Poetry Posse 2020
Gail Weston Shazor * Albert Carasco * Hülya N. Yilmaz
Jackie Davis Allen * Caroline Nazareno * Eliza Segiet
Alicja Maria Kubterska * Teresa E. Gallion * Joe Paire
Kimberly Burnham * Shareef Abdur – Rasheed
Ashok K. Bhargava * Elizabeth Castillo * Swapna Behera
Tezmin Ition Tsai * William S. Peters, Sr.

The Year of the Poet VII
April 2020
Featured Poets
Rohini Behera * Mircea Dan Duta
Monalisa Dash Dwibedy * NilavroNill Shoovro

Carlos Saavedra Lamas ~ 1936

The Year of Peace
Celebrating past Nobel Peace Prize Recipients

The Poetry Posse 2020
Gail Weston Shazor * Albert Carasco * Hülya N. Yilmaz
Jackie Davis Allen * Caroline Nazareno * Eliza Segiet
Alicja Maria Kubterska * Teresa E. Gallion * Joe Paire
Kimberly Burnham * Shareef Abdur – Rasheed
Ashok K. Bhargava * Elizabeth Castillo * Swapna Behera
Tezmin Ition Tsai * William S. Peters, Sr.

Now Available

www.innerchildpress.com/the-year-of-the-poet

and there is much, much more !

visit . . .

www.innerchildpress.com/antho
logies-sales-special.php

Also check out our Authors and
all the wonderful Books
Available at :

www.innerchildpress.com/autho
rs-pages

INNER CHILD PRESS

WORLD HEALING WORLD PEACE
2018

A Poetry Anthology for Humanity

Now Available

www.worldhealingworldpeacepoetry.com

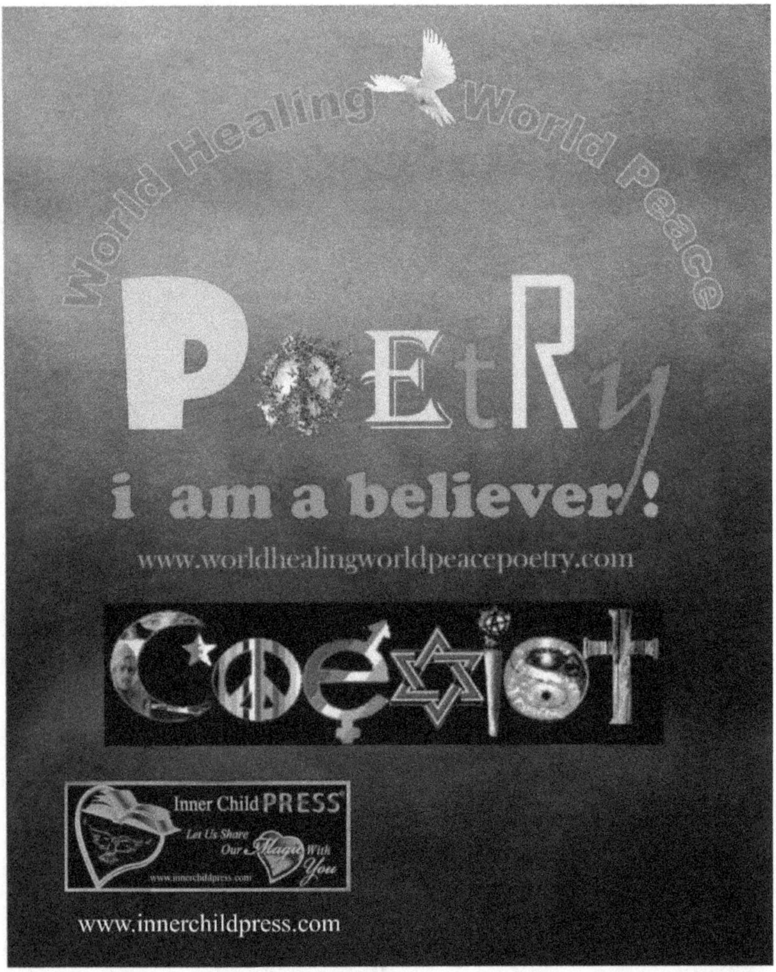

Now Available

www.worldhealingworldpeacepoetry.com

Support

World Healing
World Peace

www.worldhealingworldpeacepoetry.com

World Healing
World Peace
2018

Now Available

www.worldhealingworldpeacepoetry.com

Inner Child Press International

'building bridges of cultural understanding'

Meet our Cultural Ambassadors

Fahredin Shehu
Director of Cultural

Faleha Hassan
Iraq ~ USA

Elizabeth E. Castillo
Philippines

Antoinette Coleman
Chicago
Midwest USA

Ananda Nepali
Nepal ~ East
Northern India

Kimberly Burnham
Pacific Northwest
USA

Alicja Kuberska
Poland
Eastern Europe

Swapna Behera
India
Southeast Asia

Kolade O. Freedom
Nigeria
West Africa

Mansil Beroual
Morocco
Northern Africa

Ashok K. Bhargava
Canada

Tzemin Ition Tsai
Republic of China
Greater China

Alicia M. Ramirez
Mexico
Central America

Christena AV Williams
Jamaica
Caribbean

Louise Hudon
Eastern Canada

Aziz Mountassir
Morocco
Northern Africa

Shareef Abdur-Rasheed
Southeastern USA

Laure Charazac
France
Western Europe

Mohammad Ikbal Harb
Lebanon
Middle East

**Mohamed Abdel
Aziz Shmiris**
Egypt
Middle East

Hilary Mainga
Kenya
Eastern Africa

Josephus R. Johnson
Liberia

www.innerchildpress.com

This Anthological Publication
is underwritten solely by

Inner Child Press International

Inner Child Press is a Publishing Company
Founded and Operated by Writers. Our
personal publishing experiences provides
us an intimate understanding of the
sometimes daunting challenges Writers,
New and Seasoned may face in the
Business of Publishing and Marketing
their Creative "Written Work".

For more Information

Inner Child Press International

www.innerchildpress.com

'building bridges of cultural understanding'
202 Wiltree Court, State College, Pennsylvania 16801

www.innerchildpress.com

~ fini ~

www.ingramcontent.com/pod-product-compliance
Lightning Source LLC
LaVergne TN
LVHW011153080426
835508LV00007B/374